Night

Volume II

A Philosophy of the Last World

Night

Volume II

A Philosophy of the Last World

Jason Bahbak Mohaghegh

Winchester, UK
Washington, USA

JOHN HUNT PUBLISHING

First published by Zero Books, 2022
Zero Books is an imprint of John Hunt Publishing Ltd., No. 3 East St., Alresford,
Hampshire SO24 9EE, UK
office@jhpbooks.com
www.johnhuntpublishing.com
www.zero-books.net

For distributor details and how to order please visit the 'Ordering' section on our website.

Text copyright: Jason Bahbak Mohaghegh 2021

ISBN: 978 1 78904 941 1
978 1 78904 942 8 (ebook)
Library of Congress Control Number: 2021943602

A CIP catalogue record for this book is available from the British Library.

Design: Stuart Davies

UK: Printed and bound by CPI Group (UK) Ltd, Croydon, CR0 4YY
Printed in North America by CPI GPS partners

We operate a distinctive and ethical publishing philosophy in
all areas of our business, from our global network of authors to
production and worldwide distribution.

Contents

Introduction: Eight Principles (By Nightfall)

Principle 1: Night as Mood (atmosphere; zone)

An old philosopher, at a point when he was aged and no one was listening closely to him anymore, said that there was a single concept, a single idea, that philosophy never had the courage to confront, because it is the most treacherous, the most perilous axis of thought: Mood. This is what makes Night such a disturbing yet elegant topic: for it is the Master of Moods. Stated otherwise, Night possesses the ability to construct entire atmospheres, which is a miraculous yet also diabolical touch: it can carve out micro-worlds or zones of experience that never should have existed (meaning that they belong outside the dominant regimes of reality).

Principle 2: Night as Distortional Space (the turn)

One need only grasp how almost all spatial settings are drastically altered by the nocturnal onset: on the natural side, we can picture the powerful new sensations that arise from spending the night in the forest, the desert, the jungle, the sea, the island, the hills, the ice tundra, or staring into outer space. In terms of constructed or artificial sites, we can picture the city at night, the garden, the labyrinth, the balcony, the library, the laboratory, the cellar, the dungeon, the bridge, the rooftop, or the hotel room. A thousand tales can be formed around the particular intricacies of inhabiting these interior and exterior arenas at Night, and how the after-dark distorts essentially everything that falls beneath its blanket, like those medieval alchemists who studied strange methodologies of the turn so as to wrench things into something other than what they were supposed to be.

Principle 3: Night as Forbidden Aesthetic
(the sub-tradition)

The Argentinian writer Jorge Luis Borges once composed a very startling yet profound statement when he said: "Praised be the nightmare, for it reminds us that we have the power to create Hell." There is a certain attribution of forbidden creative will here that supposedly emerges only from nocturnal recesses, and it is not overstepping to assume that certain typologies of consciousness do arise specific only to Night—just as one can note the distinct types of poetic traditions that are born from cultures which experience varying climates or topographies: the poetics of the mountain versus the tropics, the poetics of the rainstorm versus the poetics of famine, the poetics of extreme heat versus extreme cold versus locations with fierce wind or 6 months of darkness. Idiosyncratic words are invented by the necessity of being submerged in these disparate conditions; specialized rhythms and intonations are devised under the influence of different elements.

Thus to provide some intriguing examples showing that this is almost a primordial intuition, one can cite two long-standing Night traditions that have lasted over many centuries: the first refers to classical music in Iran, which ties back to ancient rituals of mourning and burial, where there are certain modal systems and scales that are only supposed to be played between the hours of midnight to 4 am, and the great masters observe this code quite strictly, allowing those melodies to be attempted only in the after-dark hours because they presumably belong to that temporality alone. And the second example is from Japanese storytelling, where there is a certain form of narrative (sometimes tied to the folklore surrounding ghosts and otherworldly creatures) that is only recited in that same post-midnight duration. In both instances, then, Night remains connected to an exclusive or at least deeply private modality of art and perception.

Principle 4: Night as Myth (god-concepts)

To that degree, one can even return to those complex ancient mythologies and god-lineages described in the first volume of this project wherein hereditary trees of the first Night-deities were arranged with striking implications: to reiterate a single example of these strands, we consider the Greek description of how the originary force of the universe, Chaos, allegedly gives birth to four children: earth, the underworld, darkness, and night. For our purposes, Erebos (darkness) and Nyx (night) marry and have two offspring, the brothers Hypnos (god of sleep) and Thanatos (god of death). Hypnos then bonds with Pasithea (name meaning "acquired sight," as in the goddess of hallucinations). Together they live by the sub-legendary River Lethe (forgetfulness) in a cave surrounded by opium poppies and they rest on a grand bed carved of ebony. They eventually have three children called the Oneroi (the three gods of the dream): together their powers converge to form dreamscapes, their names being Morpheus (shape), Phobetor (fear), and Phantasos (phantom). Hence we note that such cosmologies were the first philosophical attempts to analyze Night; they were interpretive chambers utilizing such narrative storytelling of divinities to embody elaborate conceptual constellations that associated after-dark temporalities with chaos, sleep, death, hallucination, forgetting, fear, spectrality, etc.

Principle 5: Night as Escape (the corner, the zero-world)

Nevertheless, we find the same overarching supposition across most traditions of nocturnal-thinking: that Night is radically unbound and amorphous. It can swing like a pendulum from catastrophe to ecstasy and a thousand shades in-between, a principle that stretches into almost every domain of the human encounter with Night, including that of the child's imagination. Just revisit their bedtime stories and lullabies, and the half-gruesome, half-enthralling genre of fairytales most of which are set against a theater of Night and which mix awful imagery with astonishing senses of adventure. In an experimental current of psychoanalysis, this is what the thinker Gaston Bachelard called spheres of "intimate immensity" (which are like little trap-doors or escape-hatches from the everyday that restore to a kind of zero-world), and the best way to understand this performatively is how children or animals at play often enjoy embedding themselves in secluded places like corners, closets, attics, or when they build tents or forts to enclose themselves, or even simply hide beneath the covers or under the bed. There is a certain rapture gained from locating these tunnels or corridors of disorientation.

Principle 6: Night as Unreality (vertigo, carnival)

What this tells us even more crucially is that Night holds a particular key to unlock states of unreality. This is a staggering floodgate or Pandora's Box to open; it is the key to the Night's vertigo and carnivalesque quality, that cirque-like makeshift world of tents, sideshows, and rides: for it means that to study Night with any precision we must develop highly acute counter-philosophies of The Dream, The Nightmare, The Fantasy, The Vision, The Hallucination, The Simulation, The Mirage, The Apparition (ghost, shadow), The Memory, The Illusion, The Story, The Trance, and The Lie. Each of these unreal conditions has its own entanglement and orchestration of other themes related to Night, including those of desire, nothingness, delirium, confusion, wonder, monstrosity, solitude, cruelty, and oblivion.

Principle 7: Night as Host (personae, cast of characters)

And just to complicate things further, we have talked already about the potential spaces of Night and the conceivable concepts of Night (pointing to the kind of experiences or affects that are generated by its dark folds), but we can go another step to include a whole host of characters that are closely affiliated with Night as well. These are identities or figures whose entire destiny hangs in the balance of whether or not they can learn to navigate the nocturnal, almost like those martial artists who used to practice on cliffs with blindfolds. We must consider how Night enlists its own host, its own brood and progeny.

THE TRAVELER is a figure of constant movement. They perceive Night as a series of gateways, passages, and mapped paths through darkness. The traveler's concepts: wandering, encounter, and boundlessness. The traveler's intentions: to cross borders and enter foreign territory after foreign territory.

THE BEGGAR is a figure who crouches throughout alleyways and beneath bridges. They perceive Night as the time when vagrants rule the city streets, when those of outcast status take over the world of concrete. The beggar's concepts: drifting, survival, and neglect. The beggar's intentions: to persist through unbearable cold and loneliness; to risk existing on the outside and at the limits.

THE INSOMNIAC is a figure of extreme restlessness. They perceive Night as either a torture-chamber or a secret looking-glass onto the world while others descend into stillness. The insomniac's concepts: waking, frenzy, and vigilance. The insomniac's intentions: to endure the after-hours and thereby take consciousness beyond absolute midnight.

THE PROPHET is a figure of sacred communication. They perceive Night as the vessel for divine voices and ascend mountains to receive visions of salvation or apocalyptic destruction. The prophet's concepts: the chosen, the promise, and the future. The prophet's intentions: to deliver the final message, and bear witness before doomsday.

THE DRUNKARD is a figure of sensual heights. They perceive Night as a time of laughter, gathering, and indulgence, when tastes grow more alive and the festival begins. The drunkard's concepts: pleasure, excess, and numbness. The drunkard's intentions: to attain blind delight; to lift their glasses in honor of the permanent banquet.

THE MADWOMAN is a figure of deranged thoughts. She perceives Night as a reflection of the mind's own turbulence, a crystal ball peering into the layers of mania, delusion, euphoria, paranoia, and obsession. The madwoman's concepts: chimera, suspicion, and multiplicity. The madwoman's intentions: to become fractured like the many glass shards of a broken mirror; to shatter reality into infinite fragments.

THE CRIMINAL is a figure of lawless talents. They make alliances with Night to shield themselves from detection, entering and exiting forbidden places and thieving whatever objects are vulnerable to their cruel intelligence. The criminal's concepts: cunning, stealth, and violence. The criminal's intentions: to master invisibility; to revel in accursedness; and to threaten the order of things.

THE RUNAWAY is a figure of abandoned pasts. They perceive Night as a window of escape, trading their old identities for new spheres of possibility. The runaway's concepts: departure, distance, and cynical freedom. The runaway's intentions: to leave behind former worlds; to tread elsewhere and faraway.

THE REBEL is a figure of subversive dreams. They perceive Night as a theater of covert operations, underground meetings, and great conspiracies. The rebel's concepts: negation, outrage, and sabotage. Their revolutionary intentions: to overthrow regimes of power; to acquire something combining justice and revenge; to radically transform all that exists.

THE SORCERER is a figure of ancient incantations. They exploit the Night's silence to devise words that will turn things against themselves; they speak in diabolical tongues and seek unnatural abilities. Their magical concepts: transformation, enchantment, impossibility. The magician's intentions: to hypnotize at will; to place everything under unbreakable spells. **THE MYSTIC** is a figure of enigmas and bewilderment. They ponder material and cosmological riddles; they take tranquil steps into the unseen and hidden realms. The mystic's concepts: ritual, eternity, and (un)knowing. The mystic's intentions: to pierce through the concealed origins and destinies of things; to navigate the fine line between truth and illusion.

THE STORYTELLER is a figure of perfect diversion. They sit up at Night and prey upon others' curiosity, using poetic images to suspend them across fictive horizons. The storyteller's concepts: imagination, tone, and forgetting. The storyteller's intentions: to kill time as time kills us; to distract the entire earth with a single epic or legend.

Principle 8: Night as Neo-Madness (the hallucinatory, the otherwise)

Is it too much to ask that Night helps us break the prime law of reality by dreaming up still-unborn forms of madness? Do the writings and images of Night allow us to project perception forward into the alleys of imaginative possibility, conceiving an experimental method whereby thought itself becomes a narrative plaything (following a "choose your own adventure" model)? In essence, to ask what lies beyond the known outer limits of delirium and derangement.

It is no easy business to let Night supersede the categories of schizophrenia, mania, neurosis, delusion, hysteria, paranoia, melancholia, and obsession by allowing lunacy to enter those prismatic chambers of conjecture and hypothetical reinvention never seen before. A Pandora's Box of inexistent psychoses or hidden labyrinth of consciousness. To achieve this end, we must resurrect some of the darker visionaries of the past centuries from across the world to ask what they might have experienced otherwise (shadow-diagnosis), abandoning analysis of "actual" syndromes in order to turn their words/sensations elsewhere (toward our own prisms of neo-madness). For instance, what visions emerge when one ties melancholia (radical sadness) not to obvious psychoanalytic categories of trauma or loss but to foreign categories like color, tactility, altitudes, or atmospheres? That is, the one who falls tormented at the sight of the color purple, or agonizes at the touch of silk, or cries underwater or while walking along a skyscraper's edge. No longer the interpretation of dreams, but rather the dreams of interpretation (bordering on hallucination).

There is a certain figure of Night who surpasses the conventionally-feared lunatic: not merely the fool who blurts out the public secret (the buried unspoken of the unconscious) but the one who speaks the fresh-terror neologism (that most threatening image which one does not even know exists, did not fear previously, never repressed or anticipated in any form). This inventive will is the stuff of absolute fragility.

Accordingly, the book revolves around four primary chapters that each explore a certain thematic nexus of nocturnal experience—Night and Space; Night and Silence; Night and Violence; Night and Secrecy—alongside four short interlude chapters that present a particular figure, object, or phenomenon (The Mirror, The Fire, The Fallen, the Pretender). Within this spectrum, many doors will fling open wide that test the limits of sanity and insanity, reality and unreality, the beginning and the end: for to enter Night is no less than to devise a philosophy of the last world.

Part I

Four Essays on Night

Chapter 1

Night and Space

(Five Rooms at the End of the World)

There are those nights of rare existence when certain rooms open to us, rooms of a more deranged intimacy where we can tempt the last boundary of experience: to disappear forever. Thus the art of disappearance begins from the construction of an interior space—a single shack, corner, underground—where we bisect ourselves into two opposing figures: the trespasser and the nemesis. Function of the trespasser: to steal power from this temporary domain. Function of the nemesis: to dissolve whoever enters into thin air. And it is Night that stages this contest; it is in nocturnal hours alone that we seek the hiding-place that turns us toward hiddenness itself (the forgotten, the incognito): these farthest rooms of the earth, built to suit the farthest nights of being, though their remoteness transpires right within our midst.

We will therefore follow a sequence of five world authors of Night, glancing quickly at their conceptual configurations while also noting the three unique domains of spatial enclosure in each display of storytelling and poetics.

First Night (of the purgatorial future)
Interior Spaces: the bedroom; the screen; the city

Everything, finally, unfolded in a place resembling a deep, inaccessible fissure. Such places open secret entries into darkness in the interval between midnight and the time the sky grows light. None of our principles has any effect there. No one can predict when or where such abysses will

swallow people, or when or where they will spit them out...
The deepest darkness of the night has now passed. But is this
actually true?

Haruki Murakami[1]

The First Night suspends us in the aerial camera view of a
futuristic city, the setting of Haruki Murakami's *After Dark*,
where Night itself plays the main character, guiding a strange
plot of barely-intersecting events and figures between the hours
of 11:00 pm and 4:00 am. However, scattered throughout this
textual universe of urban contours and nocturnal meetings
are short interludes that take us into the heart of a lone
bedchamber: it is something like a bare hotel room located
somewhere in the bad lands of a metropolis; the lights have
been turned off and a young woman rests in a deep unnatural
sleep upon a single mattress, her slumber being the work of
some unknown diabolical force, and across from her motionless
body a television flickers with the live video feed of yet another
empty room; at its center, an ominously masked man sits on a
chair. He is watching her intensely and pulling her gradually
through the screen to the other side of the virtual. Thus we
are confronted with a disturbing tension: we must bear semi-
omniscient witness to Night as the site of abduction, and yet
we are not allowed to interfere (all are purgatorially stranded).

The Bedroom: It is the workshop of technological sorcery, a
minor island amid the infinity of crisscrossing districts, alleys,
and all-night clubs beyond its four white walls. This bedroom
is also where we readers are converted into insomniac voyeurs
while she remains hostage to absolute somnolescence: we cannot
speak to her nor influence the procession of events, but rather
must observe at close distance this reverse-divination system
where gods move backward (from emergence to vanishing).

The Screen: It is the separating curtain that functions both
as barrier and portal between the so-called real and those

zones of utopian reproduction, digital recording, and immortal circulation through which once-palpable beings become floating images. The screen thereby reconciles the ancient problematic of the inside and the outside by serving us this new riddle: one must first insulate oneself in order to abandon the world (sinking into palest abstraction), like those many fairy tales tried to instruct us long ago, each filled with immersive adventures (into the forest, the closet, the well, or rabbit-hole) that always led to some soul-stealing affair.

The City: It is the ultimate diversion—its grand spectacle of noise, artificial light, and consumptive excess are all just distractive particles meant to conceal the alchemical work of this one room...where a resting sacrifice finds herself pulled through chasms of eventual absorption. Before dawn, she will become permanently entrapped in the blank static of the simulated; she will lose herself to the evening of the machine, the invention, and the faceless intelligence that wants our human throne. Thus the after-dark streets teach us another crucial paradox about this futuristic concept of Night: sometimes the most impersonal spheres are required (the modern cityscape) to execute the most personal violence (existential theft).

Second Night (of the ancient ritual)
Interior Spaces: the library; the labyrinth; the ruin

Throughout the course of the generations
men constructed the night.
At first she was blindness;
thorns raking bare feet,
fear of wolves.
We shall never know who forged the word
for the interval of shadow
dividing the two twilights;
we shall never know in what age it came to mean

the starry hours.
Others created the myth.
Jorge Luis Borges[2]

The Second Night allows a certain time-travel across the frontiers of imagined antiquities, for which the later hours operate as windows into an exotic pseudo-history: their spatiality is that of the unbound figment; their temporality is that of the never-transpired past. And so it is that Jorge Luis Borges rises to the occasion of his own prophecy above (to 'create the myth') by slipping actual names/facts of eclipsed civilisations and elapsed eras beneath the layers of his own fictive projections and embellishments. Such is the ultimate gesture of shadow-play: to fantasize archaic twilights, all the while himself slowly going blind (toward perpetual nightfall). And so it is that we detect three recurring interior realms situated throughout his short stories—the library, the labyrinth, and the ruin—each of which takes on dynamic silhouettes and cryptic morphologies when handed over to those ancient nights that had never happened. In "The Library of Babel," rogue seekers come from far and wide to search the endless shelves by candlelight, each looking for that skeleton-key answer that will fulfill all questions (though going perplexed by its futility). In "The House of Asterion," a lonely minotaur recounts his tragic fall from royal bloodlines into the demented architecture of the maze, where he endures a destiny of wandering, solitude, and beastly cruelty (until surrendering himself to a death-drive). In "Circular Ruins," a mystic returns to a jungle clearing filled with sacred debris where he dreams a young boy from nothingness—testing the fringes of perception and materiality by willing him piece by piece, organ by organ (the pulsating heart, the skeleton, the eyelids) into molded incarnation, only ultimately to realize that he himself is the apparition of some other magi's speculative flames. All three stories take place in ancient nights; all three are full of ritualistic turns that reveal fate as something shape-shifting, enigmatic, or deviously obscure.

The Library: It is the great seducer of mind and curiosity—sages, elders, and seers traverse its columns and sift through its endless pages; they carry torches to illuminate its ever-stretching aisles and hunch their backs, lugging heavy volumes from table to table, never realizing that this desired Night of the one true word is in fact the Night of the lost cause. For this Library is the abyss of the illegible: they enter as readers; they take their last breath as readers still. It is where interpretation goes to die, at the outer edges of exasperation; it is where thought perishes by sheer geometry.

The Labyrinth: It is where we meet the isolated one—half-man, half-bull—whose miraculous hybridity is devalued into an object of stigma and sadistic gamesmanship. He boasts of his noble lineage; he boasts of his minimalist tastes (not a single piece of furniture), and how he has mastered the elaborate circularities of his home. He tells us that he often splits himself into two identities in order to gain company, chasing himself around corridors or flinging himself masochistically from heights until his curved horns and heaving animal torso are left covered in blood. Nevertheless, none of these sad descriptions of long solitary nights can conceal the fact that people scream in horror at the mere sight of him, and that he devours nine men every 9 years by command of a mad king who marvels as he feeds. So it is that the labyrinth is where we discover the radical torment of the perfect killing-machine.

The Ruin: It is where otherworldly projects are escorted carefully into the world, as visionary elders lay tables for their rites of astonishment, metamorphosis, and manifestation. He kisses the dust beneath him before entering into vertigo; he hallucinates the formation of arteries and veins that give rise to a child's physiology; he mouths certain spells silently and sways below the full moon. Later, he teaches the child the secrets of the fire cult and its singular delirium. Thus the Ruin is where forbidden appearances become flesh and bone, as the tears of a crying mystic give rise to the most intricate practices of conjuration, thereby tying Night back to those etherealities that walk and breathe among us.

Third Night (of totalitarian dystopia)
Interior Spaces: the warehouse; the hallway; the cell

What happened then? I don't remember. Lost in the night of time. (smiles) But he wasn't so innocent.
Griselda Gambaro[3]

The Third Night begins by malevolent invitation: we arrive at an aristocrat's gated estate in the middle of the woods (resembling a vampire castle) or at a metallic warehouse (resembling an industrial storage facility). Such is the setting for the macabre political play of Griselda Gambaro's *Information for Foreigners*, where we ticket-holding visitors are given specific passwords and clear regimented guidelines that are nonetheless coated in arbitrariness, for they are employed simply as levers of domination and exclusion. This place is where those literally 'disappeared' are held, an entire generation of alleged rebels wrested from their homes in the middle of the Night and subjected to procedures of extraction, coercion, and erasure. A guide appears at the door's threshold to divide us into groups and take us on a tour of this place of torture and untimely executions: its architecture unfolds in sinuous trajectories, gallery upon gallery, like a haunted house or the freakshow of an ill-sitting carnival (for all is obscenity here).

The Warehouse: It stands like a fortress or citadel of grave proportions, announcing the symbolic authority of some regime (the overlords) who nevertheless enjoy playing out their sickly pleasure-principles in a sort of decadent theater. This reveals to us what we have always intuitively known (from fables of the emperor's clothes): the state is nothing more than a ceremonial production, a conspiracy of emblems and choreographed visual tricks meant to induce paralyzing awe/control (society as magical prison).

The Hallway: It is what consolidates this grand dungeon into a series of micro-passages, all filled with the dank air of suspicion, as we experience the vice-like tightening of space around us (claustrophobic immensity). It is the triumph of a profane fractal unity, one through which brutal vertical hierarchies are somehow scattered horizontally in grim episodic arrangements. Still, the hallway also allows us a kind of criminal fluidity, a route in-between entrance and exit from each scene of forced confession, electrocution, or hanging; it reinforces our feeling of parasitic gazing and complicity all the while rushing us to the next crypto-tunnel before any trace of shame can enter our collective consciousness. For its narrowness guarantees our anonymity in the shaded background.

The Cell: It is the dead-end of being, the juncture of impasse and confinement. This is where we observe the disappearance itself, a glance into the inner sanctum where those banished from everyday life have been deposited and reminded of their extreme vulnerability. Some of the guards are lascivious in their interactions (mockery), some are cold as ice (assassination), some are emotionally reckless (rage), some are surgically precise (tyrannical rationality), but all occupy this last station of the cell with the same intent of imposing punishing immobility (nothing can be done). Thus the cell retains the solemn quality of those antechambers of the early pyramids and temples, their walls painted with iconographic journeys of the dead, though no longer reserved for pharaohs and queens (exaltation) but only for the enemy (hatred). So it is that Night belongs both to the forces of totalitarian structures and to their revolutionary saboteurs.

Fourth Night (of schizophrenic encounter)
Interior Spaces: the garden; the drawing; the asylum

One night in the sixth year of her life a dream takes her behind the tall mirror which hangs in a mahogany frame on the wall of her room...She enters and finds herself before a staircase which she climbs. She does not encounter anyone. She stops in front of a table. On the table is a small white card...then her vision appears to her for the first time: The Man of Jasmine! Boundless consolation! Sighing with relief, she sits down opposite him and studies him. He is paralysed! What good fortune. He will never leave his seat in the garden where the jasmine even blossoms in winter.
Unica Zurn[4]

The Fourth Night occurs in a temporal-imaginative crucible (the night's dream of daybreak) through which children and madwomen are brought together in an exercise of immanent pretending. So it is that Unica Zurn's *The Man of Jasmine* recounts the tale of her supposed marriage to a chimerical figure when just 6 years old, an extraordinary meeting in a grove that sends convulsions over the next decades of her life, from her surrealistic visual art to recurring psychotic collapses, drug experiments, and periods spent in and out of insane asylums. His vague presence inspires her to become increasingly obsessed with numerology (particularly the number 9) and to start devising compulsive anagrams (poems where the letters are rearranged to form other words and coded messages). And her drawings depict backdrops of wild enchanted spaces: gardens, thickets, endless vines and plants intertwined, and strange vegetal beings with many eyes and faces among them. The ideal kingdom for the Man of Jasmine. Thus she sketches the Night of a lunatic infatuation over and again.

The Garden: It is where the first trembling emits itself, the first oath sworn, both of them blameless in their promise and exchange of subtle vows. Moreover, the garden is no bygone memory: it is the prime altar of the word "yes," embodied in her lifelong attraction to snakes and serpents (she sees them everywhere), and hence a site of hypnotic delight and eternal wish-making.

The Drawing: It is where she protectively encapsulates her gentle oneiric world, holding the Man of Jasmine's profile in the simplicity of lines, amid methodologies of schizophrenic layering, amid journal parchments and canvases full of entangled trees that give refuge to his half-entrancing, half-frightening look. Thus the drawing is the space of the soft touch and the safe haven.

The Asylum: It is the last place she spots him, amid the barrage of electro-shock therapies, white robes, sedatives, and false caretakers. It is not long after that she becomes a nocturnal martyr, throwing herself from an apartment window while on short leave from the asylum, thereby fusing Night to the troubled love of the phantom and the phantasmatic.

Fifth Night (of the idol's revenge)
Interior Spaces: the land; the case; the museum

In a glass room
In a museum that squats
in a lost city that crouches
in a deserted land
on a vast continent
I live, elevated, confronting the eyes of men,
and paralyzing them.
At silence's end, I shake off
the events of time, and the
terror of the ninth century.
Idol of Nineveh

Its Master.

...In terror, tribes of the dead
make me blood offerings.
How many voices
tremble with the nightmare in the cadence
of the chant
I was called many names
Mahmoud al-Buraikan[5]

The Fifth Night sits us across from an object of adoration and catastrophe (the idol), an artifact of pagan tribes from ages of plague and legend, whose chilling form combines features of the alien, the animal, and the monster. This is the focus of Mahmoud al-Buraikan's poem "Tale of the Assyrian Statue," told from the perceptual vantage of the icon itself, force of both atrocity and survival, reward and curse, neither pure fiend nor pure savior, in whose chiseled body we sense some lurking bad sentience. Yes, we must tread back thousands of years to when those first civilisations worshiped graven images that looked nothing like human beings, far before the monotheistic-anthropomorphic reduction to a metaphysics of sameness, to the so-called savage intuition about reality itself: the universe does not resemble us, and thus its creators must also proceed from different motives, desires, instincts, tastes, and wonderments. This is what the ancestors thought of the apparent chaos that ruled their nights and of the puppet-masters manipulating circumstances of fatal consequence (floods, storms, fires, war, famine), such that all the gravity of the cosmos could be possessed in this one small thing called the idol. [Note: Does this meditation on indeterminate nights bear noting that the poem's author himself was stabbed to death one evening at home in old age by a roving band of looters?]

The Land: This is where the local idol first circumscribed its dominion, over a particular stretch of borders that marked its definitive territoriality: it belonged to only one geo-circle, its name was recited by only one people's chant, into which it poured its vital thirst and powers of rejuvenation. We can imagine the incantatory songs composed in its honor, and we can imagine the ruthless night-raids carried out beneath its stare, for the origin of any land is also coterminous with the logic of potential invasion, exile, treason, and conquest.

The Case: This is where we find the old idol held in the contemporary timescape of the poem, in a state of translucent containment behind some glass of an exhibition that offends its own prized materiality of gold, silver, bronze, rock, or marble. The case is therefore a device of humiliation (it casts into irrelevance), antithesis of the pedestal. Nevertheless, the longer we linger before the idol's peering eyes, the more we are intimidated by the creeping thought that this glass cannot hold it forever, and that perhaps it still holds enough animistic energy to crash outward and escape one night.

The Museum: This is the great modern carceral from which our entity patiently plots its revenge (angry return). The majority of the poem's verses revolve around tales of its endurance and the many centuries of insult it has suffered—the miniature figure tells of its glorious jewels and rings being stolen by caravans of thieves, of being buried beneath desert sands, of being mishandled by children, ants, and wolves, and of the hammer-marks and gaping holes now strewn across its once-smooth form. The museum is therefore the space of final grievance; its monumentality is testament to its guilty share in assuming the precursor's obsolescence, though it is from whose basements the idol will again unleash its Night of long-awaited resurgence and reckoning.

Epilogue
Five nights; fifteen interior realms

Nocturnal experience never gives rise to identical patterns: rather, its time-space opens onto a limitless hall of mirrors in which one can find all conceivable remnants and possibilities (including strands of ecstasy, captivation, fear, mystery, evil, passion, and abuse). It houses all the phobias and manias of our race, and others, our masks and invocations, playing host to whatever superstitions or rumors entertain us at a given moment.

In our epoch alone, there are countless treatments on such reflective prisms of Night:

...psychoanalysts like Gaston Bachelard have sought "those dreams of extreme night" where "the dreamer will find no guarantee of his existence."[6]

...philosophers like Maurice Blanchot have asked, "Is it at Midnight that 'the dice must be cast'?" But midnight is precisely the hour that does not strike until after the dice are thrown, the hour which has never yet come, which never comes, the pure, ungraspable future, the hour eternally past.[7]

Writers like Margaret Atwood suggest in her night poems that:

You rock in the rain's arms / the chilly ark of your sleep, / while we wait, your night / father and mother / with our cold hands and dead flashlight, / knowing we are only the wavering shadows thrown / by one candle, in this echo/ you will hear twenty years later.[8]

...and avant-gardists like Roger Gilbert-Lecomte describe dim-lit scenarios where:

a woman dozes on the roof her name is night / Ancient abandoned to the perils of intoxication / To sleep's fumbling treasons.../ The name is night she sleeps with one eye open / And all the world at stake on what she sees.[9]

No doubt, all have carved out their own special recess of the after-dark; all chase its puzzles and sub-compartmental illusions as if the whole world depends upon it (and they are right). For Night is simply the name we give to the unraveling, to the rise and fall of all things.

Chapter 2

Night and Silence

(Five Breaths at the End of the World)

In the ancient world, there were civilizations that developed valiant cosmologies binding Night and Silence. Stated distinctly, they interpreted the night's silence as the sheer collapse of reality/creation itself, such that every nightfall brought about yet another episode of universal breakdown. These ancestral figures—Babylonian, Sumerian, Egyptian, Persian, Chinese, Incan, Phoenician—would look upward and across nocturnal skies as emblems of burst seams and exploding divinities, for which all existence thereafter became susceptible to a phenomenology of the devastated and the unsutured. This is what it meant to cross the after-dark threshold: recurring, unstoppable apocalypse (the nightly falling-apart of world).

Indeed, such correlations were so salient that many of these same ancient populations began orienting elements of their cultural production around this bond between night and silence, thereby giving rise to nocturnal rites and traditions of art, music, literature, philosophy, theater, and mysticism. Thus we might attempt restoring ourselves to those so-called primal explanations of the civilizational cradle where many heard in the night's quiet the disquiet of a shattered earth. However, to fathom this excursion of absolute fragility in its contemporary sense, we must keep company with those literary figures who would engineer new versions of nocturnal storytelling in our self-professed modernity. This silence is the tongue of the unwanted birth and the untimely death; this silence is the philosophical weapon of the cunning who seek survival (or at least soft demise) in the face of violent impossibility.

So it is that we will follow five iconic figures of contemporary world literature—the Moroccan Ahmed Bouanani, the Vietnamese Vi Khi Nao, the Argentinian Alejandra Pizarnik, the French-Algerian Hélène Cixous, and the Japanese Kobo Abe— who each fashion their own subtle experiential association between such conceptual spheres (of quietude and evening). Moreover, they each traverse their own singular atmospheres— the insane asylum, the mountain, the wolf's den, the sleeping body, and the cardboard box—in order to trace the cryptic nexus between the speechless mouth and what we might call pitch-black destinies. Ultimately, these somber narrative-poetic imaginaries will help unlock something special: methodologies of untelling held by those most well-versed practitioners of night, silence, and the self-wrecking world: the necromancer, the dream-reader, the lunatic, the gravedigger, the grave-robber, the watchman, the corpse-washer, and the doomsday seer.

First Night (of the lunatic's silence)

When I walked through the large iron gate of the hospital, I must have still been alive...I hadn't bothered to turn around in the large hallway to salute life one last time. I had abruptly found myself in another silence—later I'll call it the silence of a jar—on a planet inhabited by caricatures of aging men, ghosts cloaked in coarse linen, happy as trees or rocks, resigned even to their vomit.
Ahmed Bouanani[10]

Ahmed Bouanani's *The Hospital* is a truly awful beginning in that it reveals the awful nature of all beginnings. The plot revolves around the admittance of a nameless man into an institution for the terminally sick (mental, physical, psychological, existential) that blurs half-amnesic memories with the afterlife. The building's facade is covered in overgrown vegetation; its rooms

25

are filled with patients of unspecified afflictions who often meet sudden deaths. They are administered dubious treatments and left to roam the gardens alone, each night turning into the alliteration of a thousand identical nights, and the narrator himself trapped in a half-conscious rambling between aura and allusion that talks back to the silence of the hospital itself.

Here Being's inception is itself a disease housed in the terrible hallways and cells of an asylum—a zone of drawn-out, silent pain and occasional piercing shrieks where the origin punishes the originated for its own pathology. The genesis thereby turns genocidal at each bend.

The very first lines operate like an initiation rite, as the newest patient arrives at dusk to traverse the final destination they will ever know. Enter Oblivion: this will be the last place to ever hold them. Each step further seals their imprisonment within a bleak evermore, the poor eternality of "another silence" that resembles those butterflies pinned down for display in some sadistic collector's jar.

But what are the design specifications of this site where the lunatic is sent to be given their sullen dispensations (becoming-suffocated)? We learn several things at the very outset: Firstly, that the hospital is an iron-curtained territory, which like most gateways possesses the dual function of keeping the chosen in and the unwanted out, and which therefore hovers like a sovereign citadel kept separate from the outside world. This means that the immense door at the hospital's entrance represents a certain exclusivity and indifference; it warns that the realm within does not function according to any known rules of the everyday but rather follows its own autonomous regulatory program of the everynight. This desolation-procedure is protected by a wall, and behind the wall happen things that could manifest nowhere else. Secondly, the barrier's crossing elicits a strange existential ambivalence whereby one becomes increasingly unsure of their own status within the hierarchies of the living, the non-living, the half-alive, and the living-dead. The narrator's self-doubting expression—"I must have still been alive"—is evidence of the one whose pulse no longer beats according to any stable ontology. The vital is dimmed beyond recognition; the body descends into a state of sulking animation. And to compound the inmate's torment further, we are told that they are not allowed even a single farewell ("salute") to their former existence while marching beneath the grand domes of this lethargy-sphere: instead, their exodus is like those godforsaken figures in religious tales who are commanded never to look back for fear of turning into salt pillars or suffering decapitation at the hands of mystery-cults. Lastly, we are given clues as to the ultimate aim of this place of removal and muted cries: that it turns one into "the caricature," a disastrous shade-semblance that still appears intact (the hollow shell) while altogether gutted of soul, sensation, and fury. "Resigned," the narrator slurs: this is a new, otherworldly degree of surrender (no despair; no feeling whatsoever) for which one simply staggers alongside their own nothingness.

In another opening passage, these ghosts of another planet are likened to the image of a waterlogged corpse being washed up by the tides: "To those watching, a drowned body rejected by the waves takes on the attributes of a monster—you turn away in disgust, or else observe at a distance, silent and respectful."[11] Why does the silence of this dank form, flung casually onto the sands in awkward distension, cause such a perceptual disturbance for the onlooker? Perhaps there are many reasons, first among which is that it brings us into naked confrontation with the temporality of the too-late: in effect, that our discovery comes at an hour of pure uselessness, like that messiah who shows up to save the world 3 days after Armageddon. Our stare upon this bloated sack of a once-being is hence the desperate gaze of futility itself; it paralyzes action and hangs the individual will by its ankles in the chamber of the ridiculous. Anything to be done at this stage can chalk itself up to the non-urgency of the whenever. Next, the problematic posed by the drowned is that its mangled husk serves as a reminder of the prospect of a bad death: in effect, that not all experiences of finitude are marked by smooth gliding paths into expiration. Here we have the evidence—an uncaring and uncared-for thing whose last breaths were consecrated by those poor choreographies of writhing, gagging, flailing, choking, and finally slackness. This one did not greet their demise while fast asleep in a soft bed in their old age; this one went down wrong. Likewise, the narrator reflects on the horror of our own imagination at the "multitude of creatures that fiercely tore into its skin and eyes," which disrupts our sensibility of anthropocentric dominance over earthly matters: rather, beyond that last conscious gasp fighting the surf we become open harbors for the sea's dismissed pantheons—anonymous playthings of foam, seaweed, and crabs who curl themselves into our hair and make homes of our listlessness.[12] And this is the same desired result of the hospital as well: to convert all entrants into hospices themselves (the worst theory of dwelling), no longer determining agents but rather unresisting surfaces for the over-determined—whatever lies beyond even passivity and idleness, those vectors of a graceless event of the post-exhausted.

Nevertheless, it is a standard lesson of primal myths that great powers or treasures are often found buried in the most misfortunate places (whale's belly; dragon's lair; underworld), and so it is that the hospital's coagulations of night and silence help bestow their own special privilege: something we might call a *death-accompaniment*. Listen to the odd intimacy with which the narrator describes this new alignment: "I rub shoulders with death every day, that's why I no longer fear him...He doesn't hide in dark corners, behind parapets, under beds, in humid, stinking latrines—he joins us at the dinner table, he laughs along with us, he shares our madness, then he leads us to our beds the same way you'd try to tuck in a mischievous child who refuses to go to sleep."[13] This companionship goes far beyond the first premise of endowing fearlessness before death, for taken to its exceptional limit we find another possibility for those who call annihilation friend: to beckon the latter forward and request favors, and thus bring the dying upon whatever one wishes. To cleave a double-edged solidarity that imposes non-solidity for all others, an affection that disaffects whoever else strays too close (to being picked): to speak in a lexicon that silences all the rest.

Second Night (of the climber's silence)

[My father and I sit together in silence and in blankness. I have no clue as to how to help my father. My father's state of mind is completely blank and he is hardly being despondent about it. I allow my thoughts to quiet down. I gaze up at my father. The sun has not climbed over the earth. Thus, I sit in the darkness with my father. The sun must be sitting at the bottom of the earth waiting just like us for an opportunity to climb up. Sitting in the darkness with my father has taught me several things. The silence is hypnotic and mesmerizing.] Vi Khi Nao[14]

Vi Khi Nao's "The Boy and the Mountain" is a piece somewhere between short story, prose poem, and mystical treatise that projects both night and silence into an elocution of doom. Her narrative observes a father and son advancing night-ward across the rocky edge, saying little in order to conserve breath, but with the ever-present understanding that the father's intent is to "lean into the mountain and pass away" upon reaching the top. The mountain is therefore the epitome of a damnation-camp, and all its climbers converted into doomsday seers, deploying its atmospheric qualities (jaggedness, solitude, vertigo) in order to consummate a patricidal finale.

The child's first association is between silence and blankness, for the thin open air of the mountain is an evacuation-ether that leads consciousness into registers of the monotone and the neutral. Here thought no longer troubles itself, and the internal voice sounds increasingly like the indifference of an operator's transmitted message across a public address system. This flat calibration is the necessary frequency of doom itself—"We sit in silence, my father and I. I believe we are doomed"—though it is not devoid of affect or mood, for we are told that "the silence is hypnotic and mesmerizing."[15] It is simply an ecstasy unanchored to a knowing subject, as the "I" loses itself gradually in the fog of a fatal enchantment. And it is an infinitely permissive state, for this subordination to the mountain's immensity allows one to interpret its blank silence as a kind of command toward all actions: "Mother, I know you have been unresponsive. I have taken your silence as approval," the father says.[16] Anything can transpire now; all delusional whims are justified; all inferences are blessed and sanctified by the non-intervention of the colossus. Kill, die, betray, avenge, ascend, or descend: she has affirmed every outcome; she has unleashed the world to the night of inexorable apophenia (the perception of meaningful patterns between disconnected things), all angulations becoming viable within this sacred geometry of an unanswering force.

How does the mountain lure child and father toward that narrow precipice of the fallen? It is possible that the massive natural form in fact represents a kind of schizophrenic time, in the sense that some lesser-read contemporary studies ascribe the common symptom of hearing voices to a short temporal lag or dissonance. More precisely, the schizophrenic consciousness hears its own thought in a slight delay, echo, or loop that then causes it to misrecognize inner discourse as an outer imposition (infiltrating whisper of the other), such that a simple split-second lapse in synchronicity with the so-called "real time" of thought engenders a suspicion of being under siege by suggestive strangers, gods, demons, enemies, etc.[17] The monologue becomes an uninvited dialog that they cannot map back to themselves, perhaps linked to a certain tachypsychia (accelerated mind) which occurs during experiences of terror (note the slow-motion effect of near-death encounters). Hence, we can start considering the mountain itself as a chronic nightmare-machine that spikes situational awareness to the point that thought races while time drags/elongates, warping one's sensorium to the extent that even Father observes its dissociative spell: "Talking feels like the fall of footsteps, not necessarily with our feet, but with our mouth."[18] Accordingly, what remains is the neo-functionality of the being-turned-inside-out...where all sentiments pour forward as persuasions from some life-threatening beyond.

Still, let us not forget that this tale is based on a subtractive formula (that one will not leave this place). So it is that the climber must inhabit the vision of the doomsday seer in the final stride, welding silence and night into a hanging fixture of travesty. For this, we must turn to the last lines of the work describing the father's helical plummet down the mountainside: "[When he collapses like that, he becomes an awkward ball. Before I can catch him, he tumbles down the mountain like a tumbleweed. I watch father twirl and twist and descend. Poor father, so circular and destroyed in motion.]"[19] These bracketed asides comparing the father's likeness in death to a tumbleweed or ball is not a cruel intonation: in fact, it is the supra-horrific clearance of all cruelty by doom. We are amid a new silhouette of passion that only those old pagan shamans apprehended, one that fuses the magisterial and the farcical into a single articulation (for these are what the gods of remoteness sound like). She recites the misshapen freefall of the father with unblinking, distant eyes and a quirk-ridden tongue, her tranquility concealing a lethal absurdism neither black nor white-humored but rather of the sheer gray. She configures the writing of doom in accordance with the etymology of "petrichor" — i.e., the earthy scent of rain upon wet soil that derives from the words *petra* (rock) and *ichor* (fluid running through the veins of Greek gods). For the child relates to the mountain like those mythic warriors who somehow confiscated a divine attribute in their journeys (stole a sacred weapon, caught a fast glimpse of the god's forbidden face, or drank a drop of the deity's blood): to have taken on the demeanor of sedimentary mineral, cloud, and altitudinal calm.

Third Night (of the wolf's silence)

More from within: the nameless object that's born and turns to dust where silence weighs down like gold bars and time is a sharp wind cutting through a crevice and it is its only pronouncement. I speak about the place in which poetic bodies are made, like a basketful with girls' corpses. And it's in that place where death is sitting, dressed in an old suit and plucking a harp by the side of a doleful river, death in a red dress, the beautiful, ominous, spectral one, the one plucking a harp all night long until I fell asleep inside my dream.
Alejandra Pizarnik[20]

Alejandra Pizarnik introduces us to a host of characters and alter-egos in her poetic *extractions*: "the fearsome shadow," "the wanderer who loves and dies," "the mysterious, autonomous girls," "the night-singer." We are also told elsewhere that "Night is shaped like a wolf's scream," but before encountering the wolves let us begin by reading the above passage.[21]

What we learn from the opening selection is that her night-works are based on the logic of mortal tradeoff: namely, something must perish-unto-silence in order for something else to live. One figure's extermination provides energetic compensation to the ravenous other, readied by a poetic mechanism that operates like a border-regime charged with sacrificial ultimatums. They must administer the transfusion; they must uphold the adrenaline-pact between the many visages that populate these fragments of her *madness stone*. So it is that the rise of "poetic bodies" are won only amid the "basketful with girls' corpses," like a musical-chairs game of place-taking and elimination, all the while a reaper plays her-his sad instrument in two sets of formal vintage clothes by the water inside a dream.[22] This is the secret ritual—of simultaneous biting and circumvolution—through which "the nameless object" evolves from silence into impossible possibility.

But how do we actually gain "entrance to the temple" where such deals are negotiated? We do so by passing through a series of delicate moods that allow her "merging with the night, until dissolving naked at the opening of time."[23] The first mood is that of the *someone-trembling*—"But silence is certain. That's why I write. I'm alone and I write. No, I'm not alone. There's someone here trembling"—whereas the second mood is that of the *something-falling*—"In the silence something was falling"—which together signal the "black birds" to descend and choose their prey.[24] However, this is precisely what brings the poetic cosmos into some counter-illuminative state, toward those "luminous bodies spinning in the fog, in a place of ambiguous neighborhoods" equivalent to "silence, the silence of always, gold coins of dreams."[25] The fact that she describes this nocturnal process through the language of currency (the gold coin) tells us that there are no free rides here: rather, to hold the pen through which "word by word I write the night" is always also to write with "the color of the dead man's eyelids" (remember that the author is herself a young suicide—by Secobarbital overdose, an insomniac drug).[26]

Something ceases; something goes on. Light is purchased through willful loss. Thus, again we are taught that we must meet "the wailing women," "the absent ones," "the desperate and silent figures," "the hanged man balancing on the lilac cross," and the "refuge of dead little girls" in order to buy tickets to a light-show for the ages: "*They are listening to the place for the purpose of listening.* The night is flashing lightnings inside your mask."[27] And this means a certain allegiance—to be "in complicity with the midnight wind"—which in turn endows a certain hazardous knowledge—to "understand these signs of incandescent sadness."[28] So it is that she establishes herself as the accountant of the skyfallen, filling her ledger with tabulations of bane and sparkling emanation.

Here we enter the final paradox of an ultra-coruscated world of shadow, for the shadow is personified night and personified silence (as wisp or tendril) convened to stage an unrivaled performance: "All night he has wrestled with his new shadow."[29] This shadow-figure somehow gives off the "inimical colors united in tragedy" while also being able to hold captive the world (its play of darkness and blaze transfixes).[30] This is the sign of a critical magicality: to turn abstract existential formulae into a theater of seductive originality; to convert Being's obscurity into masquerade; to recast the tale of Death's sorrow within the colosseum of a nocturnal aesthetics.

This shadow-play also incorporates the domains of animality and the child, though compressing both impulses into a beam of fearsome will, such that the little girl rightly "fears the very young animal in the first night of the hunting season."[31] All of this reveals the author's privileging of the newcomer at all costs, in all its myriad character-variations: the novice, the fledgling, the amateur, the apprentice, the neophyte, the acolyte, the autodidact, the protégé, the prodigy. But imagine the devastating consequence when such paragons of innocence are then injected with the conceptual supplement of the animal's ruthless survival-instinct. And so the wolf's howl returns, and with it the undetected vow between silence and screaming, the beast and the infant, the shadow and the suicide.

Like those futuristic theorists who advise blowing up other planets in order to steal their energy (the violence of second suns), we find ourselves on a gameboard of calamitous or even parasitic decisions. Pieces are thrown beneath and trampled with the flick of a wrist; old cities are brought into terminal winter in order to clear way for the emergent, the imminent, and the impending ones. Night-silence is therefore also what holds court and offers testimony to *their* rights—whatever approaches, whatever gathers from afar—above the pre-existing.

Fourth Night (of the dream-reader's silence)

Models? No models: there are none where I go, the wild earth is still being invented. But while I move ahead alone in the mobile night, I perceive the signals of other nocturnal vessels passing under the same sky. It is because there is always that famous secret society, the Masonic Order of the Alert, the entirely diasporated people of borderjumpers. No one of them imitates another. But each one recognizes that the other is also called. And we hear their passwords resonate. There is not a unique password, one shibboleth. Each one has his own according to his language, and it is all the language of each that is shibboleth. The sonorous night is a caravan. Kayrawan came from Persia in the thirteenth century. And to sense that dead and surviving star-searchers share the solitude is reassuring. The solitude of each writing is always shared [*partagée*], partaken.
Hélène Cixous[32]

Hélène Cixous's *Three Steps on the Ladder of Writing* explores three supposed schools of literary imagination with close ties to the dark: The School of the Dead, The School of Dreams, and the School of Roots. The first chapter struggles with finality's handwriting-on-the-wall; the second chapter embarks on a passage into chimerical etchings of the head-on-pillow; the third chapter looks at the long-standing relation between textuality and depths or nether-worlds. However, for our purposes of tracking how "the phrase now voyages in your internal silence," we will select the middle-path of the dream-reader.[33]

The concept of voyage is paramount here, and yet from the opening excerpt we deduce that it is one without deductive practice, meaning no navigation instruments are available (maritime compasses, wind-gauges) to guide our pace. It is the obsolescence of reading the lay-of-the-land ("no models"); there is no one to ask directions from or previous footpaths to study ("none where I go"); and worst of all, it is an unfounded terrain still-under-construction ("being invented"). And yet, like those vampires who tread for centuries alone while knowing themselves bound to an unspeakable race, occasionally walking by one another in medieval forests or modern city streets with only the slightest acknowledgment of a glance or nod, the dream-readers too find themselves members of a "secret society" in which others are making similar passages. Moreover, they are all diasporic (meaning literally "splitting of the seed"); they are all expert border-crossers; they are all "inimitable" in their neo-natures; and they all aspirate in slippery or baffling syllables of the password.

What goes unmentioned here, however, is that the caravan vessel on which she muses goes hand-in-hand with the phenomenon of the *caravanserai*: namely, those temporary hangouts of the wayfarer where night-stories (both legendary and lived) proliferated under a code of silence. They were concurrently wine-taverns and hashish lounges, rest-stops and havens for outlawed music, artistry, and eroticism; they were the epicenters of transient visitation and the exchange of precious illusions. Beneath their large tents was always a hallucinatory commerce where the weary traded drunken visions, adventures, wishes, and lies, all equally protected by the guarantee of safety afforded by this roadside anti-monument. In essence, the caravanserais were each their own School of Dreams.

We observe clearly enough how this metaphor of the hideaway—one for which "something must be displaced, starting with the bed"—gradually forms a connective fabric between night, silence, and the secret.[34] This is why the author turns to a telling quotation by Clarice Lispector, in which the latter reminds us of the caravan's often-overlooked partner (the horse): "In *my* night I idolize the secret meaning of the world. Mouth and tongue, And a loose horse, running free. I keep his hoof as a fetish. In the depths of my night there blows a crazed wind that brings me threads of cries."[35] Thus the School of Dreams is uncovered through a metamorphic bell-toll, which leads us to an important qualification regarding any philosophy of silence: that there are often exclusive soundscapes, tones, indicators, or missives—like those infrasonic and ultrasonic frequency-ranges and high pitches heard only by certain species—which are experienced as fully audible to some, faint noise to others, and still totally imperceptible to others. Not all are meant to grasp: so it is that the confidentiality-modes of both night and silence create their own hierarchies and scales of access.

Lastly, by what criterion does one graduate from the School of Dreams? Perhaps it is something along the lines of honing sympathetic vibration toward those calls/waves that sabotage the mythologies of the self, for "one has to go away, leave the self... must walk as far as the night, one's own night...through the self toward the dark."[36] This would require placing the external ear canal and the eardrum's tympanic membrane in opposition to the mind's belief in itself, a movement toward what the author calls "cosmos night, where the winds of mysteries blow... [and] I myself am no more than a dream."[37] Let us not take this proposition lightly, for what does it entail to inhabit oneself as a dream? This itself first depends on one's fundamental definition of the dream and the reverberations of such dream-theories, for while certain prominent psychoanalysts leaned toward explanations of the involuntary return of the repressed (the "royal road" to unconscious trauma, compulsive desire, or residual messaging from various sub-personalities), others advanced a more radical orientation whereby the dream was a lingering relic of some pre-psychic antecedent (an enchantment-state before consciousness, identity, and the division of reality/unreality). This notwithstanding, our author of the fourth night in a single word gives us another directive altogether: for she says "I will go posthumously."[38] The dream as posthumous experience would thereby project self into the pseudo-silent afterward—where one persists only as rumor, allusion, figment, something barely spoken of or reminisced-upon from a futural someday that might never actually transpire. An alternative classification of tangibility: the dream of the hour when one becomes dream.

Fifth Night (of the gravedigger's silence):

I am getting along here with these notes, as I take shelter from the rain under a bridge. Overhead the Prefectural Highway Three crosses a canal. It is just fifteen or sixteen minutes past nine by my not too accurate watch. The dark night sky trails its skirt of rain low over the surface of the land. It has been falling since morning. Fishery warehouses and lumber sheds stretch away as far as the eye can see. There are no human habitations and no one passes by. Even the headlights of trucks coming and going on the bridge do not reach this far. A flashlight suspended from the ceiling lights the paper beneath my hand. Perhaps that is why the letters formed by my ballpoint pen seem almost black when they should be green.
Kobo Abe[39]

Kobo Abe's *The Box Man* forms a strange two-way mirror whereby the modern cosmopolis becomes the image of cosmological emptiness. We spend the entire text following a series of urban recluses who have decided to exist in cardboard boxes, living beneath bridges or shuffling in dark alleyways, with only a small window-like slit cut out to show their bloodshot eyes. These are seemingly the perfect role-players of night and silence brought together as pure negation: sallow, negligible, throwaway symptoms of the very equivocation of the world itself. Or are they livewire transistors that conduct signals of a different kind?

The more devious philosophers of these past 3 centuries have characterized the watchword for our epochal ontology (i.e. the other name of Being in this time) as Waste. But if the incommunicative box-man roving slowly through the night-city is the impersonal typification of this wasted era—withdrawn, pointless, unheard—then why does he write endlessly in frayed notebooks? Is his wretched synthetic interiority maybe not a poor asceticism of retreat but rather the laboratory for a creative instinct that can happen only within these four square walls?

Let us embark upon a double-edged theory here: writing that is the impersonation of silence, and silence that is the impersonation of writing. This is why his letters "seem almost black when they should be green," for the box-man is not a true writer in any sense of vocation, identity, or genre: he jots down notes which are replete with laundry lists of prosaic details; he notices tedious or seemingly trivial features of speed, light, tactility, proportion; he takes hermetic photographs and makes inventories of every item across each setting. Like an expert taxonomist, he encounters both objects and subjects as parts of elaborate yet boring strata, like those minds which when stumbling upon random cords start meditating on the distinctions between cables, ropes, threads, braids, chains, belts, wires, and strings, or which automatically perceive water in its triumvirate iterations of liquid, ice, and smoke, or in its specialized formulations of rain, stream, sea, spit, bubble, puddle, and wave. At first glance, this is where meaning goes to die—i.e., everything recited with the same flat-line attentiveness of the network—but what if this is not a reductive equalization or hypomimia (rigid facial masking)? What if this instead betrays a phenomenological super-paranoia whereby nothing is taken for granted, yet where every pinpoint is treated as the potential linchpin of the entire universal operation?

To watch everything indiscriminately is to enter a conditional hyper-voyeurism: to trail incidents with a measured balance of proximity (close enough to observe) and distance (far enough to remain undetected). For the voyeur is never the witness (they cannot be called upon to give testimony); they tell no one, all the while using their ironic silence to chronicle the unspoken, overlooked scenes of the world one by one. To that degree, the box-man is the ultra-conscious nobody—the ears and eyes of the unrecorded motions of this half-life in which we feign control. And his words? Again, they are the concretized textualities of silence's ventriloquism of writing and writing's ventriloquism of silence, which together fall like that never-realized imperialist weapon of "death dust" (almost developed by superpowers in the last century) meant to cover entire capitals in a blue radioactive powder.[40] Much like these hypothetical, untested methods of war, the box-man disperses his inspective gaze as a fine luminescent poison coating the cityscape at night. [Note: Remember that this author's other literary masterpiece is set against the horrendous granular backdrop of the sand dune].

This death-dust stylistics is therefore bound tightly to the logic of catastrophe, and more importantly to the temporal protocol of catastrophic experience: the countdown. Notice the tenacity of the following statement: "You flip over more than ten pages and open to a clean one. Grasping your ballpoint pen, you assume a posture for writing, but changing your mind, you look at your watch. Still 9 minutes until midnight."[41] He knows the exact hour and page number; he counts the minutes stroke by stroke. In this capacity, writing is fastidiously aware of the jaw into which it crawls; it exists as sheer prelude to the all-blanketing froth and foam of the coming demise. This is why he concurs that "Perhaps the act of writing is necessary only when nothing happens," for when the *at-long-last* occasions itself there will be only silence...silence and infinite piles of the box-man's diaries cataloging every split-second leading up to it.[42] These reports are encyclopedic and indexical because they tread the supposed fault-line of an earthquake at all instances; and the author himself is no depressive but rather a zealot whose discipline is to inscribe the unappreciated fact that we are all runaways of the open and into the box, though then flung back into the open on some startling night.

Nevertheless, it is precisely this sort of consciousness that harnesses the provisional above all others ("changing your mind"). This is why he is at once both the withheld and the invasive one; moreover, this cheaply-folded accessory latched to his back and leaving his heels exposed is less an allegory of the now's alienation and more an emblem of the always already entombed ruse of being. For the expressionless curiosities that enter the box-man's journal are in fact part of a dualistic ritual: by layering writing onto silence and silence onto writing, it makes him both the corpse-washer (putting things to rest) and the necromancer (bringing things to bare life). And then still later, when he collapses eventually into irremediable silence, he finds himself presiding over that abyss (universal encasement) for which his scribbling pen forms the shovel to act both as gravedigger and grave-robber of human thought. Here all writing becomes epitaph.

Epilogue
Five breaths; five stories of silent ends

So it is that the practice of nocturnal storytelling in world literature (the writing of untold experience) derives from a more insidious station: that of becoming the watcher of ecliptic events. These watchmen and watchwomen are the wardens of a zero-circuit; they are posted along the camouflaged periphery where some must pronounce "The End" to worlds, and always doing so in disguised, unconfessed breaths. Their hush is therefore the production of an irreproducible black transcript: like those first dusk-conscious generations thousands of years before with whom we started this chapter, who perceived in each silent hour the hints of a recanted Creation and for whom all time marked the onset of a recurring last night.

Chapter 3

Night and Violence

(Five Raids at the End of the World)

Let us consider the grave implications of the older Persian word *shabi-khun* (literally "blood-night," meaning night-raid or ambush). It is an expression of covert harm, beholden to the more dishonorable faces of war, which combines all of the most refined elements of subterfuge to guarantee its successful execution. A wicked art-form of both the highest and lowest orders, of Trojan horses and fifth columns, and a potential passcode for the meaning of futurity beyond our time.

Etymologies are Pandora's Boxes of imagination, chimera, and ruse: so it is that one of the original connotations of the word *authentic* in ancient Greek signified the "one who kills with their own hands." What would it mean, then, to build a philosophy of violence based on inauthenticity—to kill through others' hands, or to oneself kill as another? Thus we enter the dark folds of the *shabi-khun*—its twisted imagery of quiet infiltration, sleeping bodies, and slit throats—for the night-raid's protocol allows precisely that slip of mind, tongue, and sensation wherein one wills onself like a curved dagger into the world's chest (without leaving an identifiable trace behind).

Can an entire epochal fortune hang in the balance of an ancestral tactic of infliction? We will follow five articulations that place us in this special continuum of night and violence: those of conspiracy, premonition, disguise, synchronism, and fatal lull. For these are the first signposts of the night-raid: the most efficient paradigm of nocturnal cruelty ever conceived.

First Night (of the conspiracy)

One gets the feeling that, in large measure, it may come
down to a question of skill; although it is impossible to tell
what kind of skill will be involved, knitting a crack together,
perhaps, or learning how to distinguish the fault-line where
something has fractured?...Oh, we all know who could pass
through the eye of the needle without ignominy—yes, it is
the murderer—but which one of us is actually a murderer?...
Would one of us alone be sufficient to constitute the character
of the murderer, or can we succeed only if we all act together?
Giorgio Manganelli[43]

The inceptive feature of the blood-night or night-raid
configuration is that it must learn to view every dimension of
experience through a conspiratorial lens: this implies a concurrent
tendency to both interpret outer reality and to themselves
operate within prisms of immanent suspicion. In this sense,
nothing is what it seems and nothing one does is exactly what
it is: both perception and action become participants in a more
convoluted expression of will, significance, and consequence
(the distorting mirror). Indeed, conspiracy demands that one
intend misunderstanding—i.e., to become the ferryman and
peddler of a perplexed micro-verse—to the extent that others'
confusion unwittingly makes them an apprentice of the invisible
plot. Here modular curtains are drawn across the eyes; here
the five senses are tricked by misleading orchestrations of the
apparent world.

This is the initial step in any conspiratorial formulation, as it
restores that exclusive typology—what we might call immoral
intelligence—at the very heart of all definitions of evil. For
how do we analyze those who scheme and beguile on behalf
of destructive or even lethal ends? How do we acknowledge
the philosophical complexity behind such manifestations of ill-

sorted cunning that leave unconscious casualties in their wake? They are daunting, elegant, and often brilliant in their weighing of adverse effects and angles of malevolent possibility.

See *justification* [i.e., when nothing is to be trusted, existence itself becomes an amoral playing field (of the merciless game). If the night-raider is thus the exemplar of this devious perspective of the open, then all that is required are the right stratagems to move across space and time. Conspiracy is this art of undetected persuasion; conspiracy is the art of hiding the individual in the collective and the collective in the individual; conspiracy is the art of anticipation of what others still cannot discern; conspiracy is the art of working in veiled relation while appearing solitary, harmless, or undefended. Beyond this, conspiracy also justifies itself through successive micro-screens, using mediation to inflict and distance to strike closer.]

Example: Giorgio Manganelli (Italy, 1964). The aforementioned avant-garde author, who once conceived a piece titled "Literature as Deception," takes us into the chasms of a certain mindset where conspiracy is both launched and endured at all turns. He is an eccentric, with chapter titles including Simulations, Ignominy, A Few Hypotheses Concerning My Previous Reincarnations, and Disquisition on the Difficulty of Communicating with the Dead. He is a megalomaniac, prone to statements like, "It seems to me to be beyond question that I am a King."[44] But what kind of King wills conspiracies against his own land, boasting how he "fashions my palace as an endless ruin, not just as a single city but an entire region, a continent laid waste by war, disaster, unforgiving seasons, earthquakes and landslides, epidemics or millennial decadence."?[45] This is an elite orchestration of conspiratorial consciousness, for it shoots against itself like a projectile or hurled javelin, but not inwardly (resulting in paranoiac trauma) but rather outwardly (resulting in a hyper-sensitive, hide-and-seek of saboteurs). These shadow-semblances of self that break into conniving legions around him—each with their own "wastelands, castles, fortresses, absurd and senseless wars"—teach him the lesson of remaining on guard (the lookout) against the products of his own ever-factionalizing subjectivity: for to think is to apparently give rise to "further puzzling reincarnations [who] lie in wait for me."[46] Furthermore, he awards these nemeses as mercurial gifts "to my I of the coming century," all the while giving us a key clue of how to pass these endless tests of collusion and machination by "acquiring that theological hatred within which all other hatreds are to be found."[47] In essence, the conspiracy-theorist or night-raider must love to hate "these unscrupulous conspirators" of a "vile collective insanity" who judge our "voices troublesome and hostile to their ecstasies."[48] The night-raider must acquire a taste for this chronic assault of multiplying string-pullers and mapmakers, those whose intricate doctrines form diagrams of the unprincipled, in a stealth-hinged cosmos of acting alone and acting together...and for which the ravaged is always high currency.

Second Night (of the premonition)

No, no way, no one will change my being. I am Estamira here, there, and overthere, in Hell, in Hells, in heaven, fucking everywhere. These misfortunes, these parasites from the forsaken filthy earth, this accursed unholy earth, denied man as the sole conditional. The more evil I become, the worse I am. Perverse, I am not. But evil I am. Before I was born, I knew all of this. Before I had flesh and blood. Of course, for I am the margin of the world!...It will be far worse when I disincarnate.
Estamira Gomes de Souza[49]

Let us entertain a counterintuitive proposition: that premonition is what ruins expectation. Thus to say that the night-raiders attune themselves to premonitory forces is in fact to imply being on the lookout for the unexpected (contortion, slanting). This is their exceptional advantage over others: this is what makes them expert agents of the element of surprise. The skill of locating vastness within the permutational and the positional (logic of the crucible).

Whereas social bonds are often formed around momentary erosions of formal codes of behavior (vulgarity, transgressive humor), the night-raiders forge bonds of closeness around the increasing elaboration of codes (coordinated rhythms, aligned mannerisms) similar to those game-masters who marvel at one another's elevated difficulty of moves across the board. Whereas familial bonds are based on symbolic bloodlines (static heredity), the night-raiders forge bonds through co-enacted bloodshed (cumulative practice). Internal mythology vs. external trajectology. Technique, ingenuity, and displays of versatile imagination amid situations of constraint; fluidity and navigation across tightly-bound grids—and not in the absolute temporality of some given identity, but measured only at the hour when it counts most (under pressure).

Premonitory consciousness is also its own razor's edge of fanaticism, since the pure fanatic is weirdly also the perfect nihilist with respect to all other facets of existence (they worship only the one thing, at the expense of all else). So it is that the devotee in most instances constitutes the perfect rebel as well— for they obey their most narrow master, thereby breaking/ ignoring all other structures and codes. Indeed, the one who swears themselves to a single order becomes an agent of chaos to everything else that stands.

When imagining the night-raid's temperament—how it riles, calms, focuses, or incenses itself—let us consider three specific genres of premonition that have existed in almost all instances of human undergrounds: the manifesto, the prophecy, the spell. Though all cast themselves toward visionary advents of futurity, each contains its own procedural makeup, compositional method, and hermeneutic outcome. With respect to speed, the manifesto is predicated upon acceleration, the prophecy on anticipatory stillness, and the spell on slowness forming cumulative tempo. With respect to affect, the manifesto aims toward animative fury, the prophecy toward awe and reverence, and the spell toward spellbinding (through coldest strands of agitation and subduing). With respect to the resulting event, the manifesto craves revolution, the prophecy assures salvation or reckoning, and the spell leans either toward curse, healing, transformation, or decimation. With respect to its practitioner, the manifesto is often spoken by the iconoclast/leader, the prophecy by the mystic, prophet, or oracle, and the spell remains the utterance of the sorcerer. With respect to time, the manifesto positions itself at a temporal threshold of urgency (present-as-horizon), the prophecy plays moments off to messianic deferrals (later judgment), and the spell inscribes itself in circular patterns of the eventual (the already-done). With respect to space, the manifesto's domain is usually that of the subterranean rally, the prophecy situates itself on the mountain, the tablet, or the temple, and the spell emerges from within the den but then afterwards tracks itself into the nexus of the encounter. With respect to textual duration, the manifesto is composed of long yet provocative inventories/lists, the prophecy condenses itself into a single line or passage, and the spell takes shape as an assemblage of utterances simultaneously isolated (pre-apparatus) and coalesced (vortex). With respect to power, all three warp the boundaries of clarity and confusion: the manifesto through its severity and call-to-arms, the prophecy through its vagueness and enigmatic folds, and the spell through the esoteric sounds that grant it impenetrable exclusivity. With respect to orientation, the manifesto attempts unification through outrage or euphoria, the prophecy suspends one in the air of neutrality and bewilderment, and the spell dominates either through fear or enchantment. So it is that the manifesto's premonition envelops the crowd in a pedantic imperative to advance, the prophecy's premonition forms a transcendent bridge joining the beyond and the particular, and the spell's premonition motions against other, object, or world with a kind of unidirectional brutality.

Example: Estamira Gomes de Souza (Brazil, 2004). She is a figure of simultaneous calmness and tirade (introversion-extroversion reflex); she breaks between omens, boasts, profanity, and rants. For she mimics the arc of the premonitory outburst itself; she sits and stands in whirlwind formations of thought turning into cosmic sentencings. To dissect the opening quote is therefore to recognize the individual particles inherent to premonitory consciousness (as the subject epitomizes the foreboding):

See *immutability* [i.e., first, she declares that "no one will change my being"].

See *immanence* [i.e., second, she declares herself "here, there, and overthere"].

See *accursedness* [i.e. third, she declares herself the repository of "these misfortunes, these parasites of the forsaken filthy earth"].

See *evil* [i.e., fourth, she continually repeats the line "evil I am"].

See *intensification* [i.e., fifth, she warns of a growing proximity to "the worse I am"].

See *augury* [i.e. sixth, she declares herself the keeper of a pre-emptive seal ("before I was born, I knew all of this")].

See *distance* [i.e., seventh, she declares herself "the margin of the world"].

See *threat* [i.e., eighth, she declares herself "far worse when I disincarnate"].

See *rage.* [Perhaps the most crucial component of this speaking-into-imminence goes unspoken (as it is performed).

Rage is how Estamira becomes unstoppable; rage is how she both summons and wards off entities in her midst: she flies into bouts of phantom anger while unraveling theories about remote-control forces and technical divinities who have invalidated all remaining innocence. She spins predictive webs around her home and land, noting that the malediction "does not burn, it twists." And she has many tentacular names for these figments of hate who assail her in the trash heaps where she lives: at times she calls this oppositional entity "the living hypocrite" or "the scoundrel;" at other times, she calls it "the astral father," "the wiseguy in reverse," or "the punster's grudge." She relentlessly accuses it of having "seduced men and tossed them into the abyss" and promises to "expose his whole gang, knock him down." So it is that rage (horizontal axis) converts her into the summit (vertical axis) that then issues the ultimatum (vertex) between colliding worlds of power (spiral): this is the full cycle/lunge of the night-raid itself (and the premonition's spear).]

Third Night (of the disguise)

The mask, so it appears, makes possible instant dissimulation. Entrenched behind his mask, the masked person is shielded from the indiscreet inquiries of the psychologist. He has found in a moment the security of a face that gives nothing away. If the masked person can then re-enter life, and decides to adopt the life of his own mask, he readily assumes himself a master of mystification.
Gaston Bachelard[50]

Fatality's quality is often measured by its softness (like silken cloth), such that silence, swift strides, and painless inflections of the wrist are all valued criteria of the night-raid. Following the Devil whose greatest victory lies in dissuading belief in his presence (convincing others that he does not exist), so must the night-raider steal death with the lightest possible touch. This is the discipline of disguised being, like the lullaby with its paradoxical ability to import violent lyricism while soothing unto softest sleep.

We can first learn the nature of disguise from those petty criminals—the pickpocket, the stick-up artist, the chain-snatcher—who sneak up from behind and seize only mobile items of preciousness. Here the night-raid is a matter of split-second, lightweight transfers (maximal reaping in minimal scales of time and exertion). But we can also discern alternative types of disguise in more luxurious examples of twenty-first-century spectacle: namely, those new rulers of the East who are fusing avant-garde, ecological, and authoritarian projects toward the rise of pseudo-utopian capitals. Hence, today in the same desert locales where night-raids first occurred, we find dynasties building futuristic linear city-states with artificial rains/moons, holographic technology, artificial intelligence, and museums/libraries of the future. Is this a radical departure from the original tribal calculus of the blood-night or is it a super-treacherous extension of its path? No longer under cloaks of darkness but rather amid the false radiances and spotlight-effects of the virtual, do these rising metropolises only further indulge the elder violence in new smokescreens of digital light? Here the night-raid is a matter of flagrancy, grandeur, and hiding in plain sight.

What potential uses might the night-raid hold for the primeval object of the mask? For thousands of years, an artifact of old clerisies, secret societies, cult formations, warrior cultures, and costumed children, though later an implement of disgraceful violence (the bandit, the marauder, the *ninja/shinobi*). Let us follow the compartmentalized logic of the above quote in order to uncover these peculiar endowments of the mask:

See *instantaneity* [i.e., that the mask bestows a certain

"instant dissimulation," which refers to its lightning-quick capacity for covering or trafficking things into the domain of unreadability].

See *discretion* [i.e., that it baffles and runs circles around efforts at psychic penetration ("shielded from indiscreet inquiries"), trading the interior blindness of consciousness and the unconscious for a supra-conscious stare].

See *security-device* [i.e., that it serves as an emergency-measure in the state of war, one that squanders no information/advantage to the enemy ("gives nothing away")].

See *manipulation* [i.e., that the author suggests a duplicitous ability to bring the mask back into everyday reality; to continue deriving its gifts even in the night-raid's aftermath and thereby enjoy mishandling of the so-called normal spheres of life ("master of mystification")].

See *invitation*. [For what if one never really returns from the night-raid's incursion, as if the stain of virulent conflict were blotted across the mind in perpetuity? Would this not result in nothing less than a total identification with the mask? The same author tells us later that the item functions as a recurring *invitation* ("a mask asks to be worn"), from which we can deduce that its pre-eminence might result in the one who no longer employs it to shroud the authentic face but rather to engulf the original identity to the point of full dominion (becoming-mask). This is how the night-raid ultimately eludes all psyche (judgment, guilt, shame, trauma, anxiety, memory): for it inhabits the material article of pure stigma, leaving no one behind to answer for the vacant sockets and thin-mouthed aperture set in iron, stone, glass, or cloth.]

Example: Pablo Gargallo (Spain, 1915); Tomás Barceló Castelá (Spain, 2021). Two Spanish sculptors of the mask separated by a century: the first dared to chase after surrealistic paradigms of the masquerade, while the second entertains futuristic paradigms of the masquerade. However, both are trying to embezzle something through the pseudo-visage; both are sending out their masks like satellites of a certain fantastical battle in the surrounding hills and valleys. To this end, Gargallo of Zaragoza dwells in avant-garde cellars until he can one day fabricate his tetraptych series consisting of four copper-sheet masked fauns: The Faunessa with Earrings; The Faun with Beard; The Faun with Monocle; The Faunessa with Bangs. Long convex heads, part-odious and part-caricaturesque: they are both wonderful and teratoid (meaning monstrous, or tumor-like); they are changelings, at once wolves in sheep's clothing and sheep in wolves' clothing. And what might the night-raid hold in common with these mythic half-goat, half-human creatures of the feast, the festival, the banquet, and the dance? Is there some quizzical share that they both maintain in the tendency to simultaneously guide, amuse, and mislead through enchanted forests? Do their pointed ears and melodies make the same unusual pact with dissemblance (meaning to hide intentions or feelings) and waylaying (meaning to detain, interrupt, or trouble along a path)? What would it mean to say that the night-raider perceives violence as a kind of anarchistic celebration or orgiastic rite? One hundred years later, Barceló of Mallorca will take up this archaic legacy on the Mediterranean islands, crafting masks that meld antiquity and futurity in the same way that early Egyptians envisioned faces/helmets where alien and god become visually interchangeable. Sleeping Princess; Monk Robot; Ivory KAL-IX; Old Automata; Dark Lilith; Evil Baby Mask: these are the workshop models through which space-time is subordinated to the merciless philosophy of the disguise. He therefore follows in step with both science fiction and hieratic traditions—those banished priesthoods of the hoods, robes, and visors—in order to manufacture new prototypes of the icon and the anachronism.

Fourth Night (of the synchronism)

The Sahrawi women made and built everything. And at night, when we were alone with no men, we would take turns in groups to guard each other. And if we were under threat, we would go into the trenches.
Al-Khadra[51]

The night-raid partakes of a kind of *synchronism* (operational concurrence) and *synchronicity* (meaningful coincidence) for which all other discourses of relationality, collectivity, brotherhood/sisterhood, and intersubjectivity pale by comparison—stronger than history, these oaths of irregular, asymmetrical war at once possess all the faculties of the solid, liquid, and aerial.

See *life-and-death intimacy* [i.e., that to fail is to effectively kill the remaining cadre, forming themselves as a fabric, compendium, and episodic alliance of mortal stakes].

See *reactive interplay* [i.e., that they adjust themselves neo-instinctually to gliding/cutting responsively across one another, and thereby accommodate individual improvisation or extemporaneous action in the field].

See *signaling* [i.e., that they develop nuanced conduction-transmission syndicates that deliver information through atypical gestures or sensory phenomena—colors, sounds, traces, encryptions, visual cues, facial expressions, scents, passwords].

See *rotational flexibility* [i.e., that they avoid the soldiers' rank-and-file, pyramidal charging in exchange for an adaptable chain of interchangeable parts—V-formations; S-formations; flanking, looping, false perimeter, or blanketing maneuvers. This panoramic yet infra-dispensable quality renders the fighter increasingly fearless].

See *intelligence* and *espionage* [i.e., that they employ eavesdropping, stalking, spying, surveillance, bribery, rumor, persuasion, booby-trapping, and well-placed swarms of informants, decoys, or impostor-insiders to compensate for their outnumbered status].

See *shock-value* [i.e., that they stage unsavory displays— abduction, beheading, burning, mutilation, resource depletion, civilian abuses—in order to wrest enemies into attrition. The gradual wearing-down or exhaustion of reciprocal will.]

See *underestimation, overestimation* [i.e., that they exploit both their initial *underestimation* and their subsequent *overestimation*. Originally the night-raiders' influence goes discounted or even largely unknown, but later their nefarious image is prone to notoriety and exaggeration following the first attack. So do they inhabit the space of legend, whisper, and nightmare. This is how the group's synchronization (as a breathing armament) finally helps evoke the atmosphere of synchronicity (to make others see plotting in accidental-coincidental signs): their attainment of the outer degree of imputation, spoken of in dreadful innuendo, as all negative occurrences are then paranoiacally ascribed to the raiders' misdeeds. Half-scapegoat, half-boogeyman].

This is how a human pack becomes a perfectly-oiled instrument (both in the sense of music and machine), which is why the night-raiders are often able to mobilize even high-probability pain as a recruitment device (harmonization overrides loss, personifying a dance of death). It is to breathe the rarefied air of the cliffs and outlaw caves where dreams of counter-insurgency, counter-pursuit, and unconventional motion are born. Nevertheless, their synchronization is all in the service of confirming the radically circumstantial format of existence: the living for no reason, the dying for no reason. And their choreographies in fact resemble this cynical perspective: they do not march like standing armies but rather crawl, scurry, crouch, dart, and freeze in place; they are not motivated by ideological identity but rather only by the coagulating law of momentum itself.

Example: Al-Khadra Mint Mabrook (Western Sahara, 1976). She is the war-poetess of the displaced and imperially-bombarded Sahrawi people (literally "desert inhabitants") of southern Morocco. She adapts the rugged nomadic lifestyle of those Bedouin tracts into a poetics of combat and immortalizes the story of the tribal women's self-protection in the absence of their captured, slaughtered, in-hiding, or at-battle men. These women organize themselves into a barrier against the invading kings, and refuse acquiescence of their homeland by intuitively reading one another in those long nights of despair and threat. So it is that she rehearses the synchronistic modalities of the night-raid in defense of their sand-vistas, learning with great agility to "take turns" on guard or to retreat "into the trenches" when unable to withstand face-to-face confrontation. And they prevail in drawing out a grueling stalemate for all those many years, a source of true pride (given the likelihood of total erasure) for which she boasts of those that "burnt the iron of the enemy and reined them into control…set the tank alight, setting the iron on fire." Her factions are not the first blood-drawers but rather of the second-blood (by retaliation): nor does al-Khadra invoke the military terminology of blowback, ricochet, or collateral damage but rather relies upon allusions to the more primordial violence of flame (to make them choke upon their own combustible fuels). For such hardened, volatile places (the desert, the street) require the overcoming of the impoverished psychological division of conscious versus unconscious spheres. In states of war, one must never dare think something that they are unwilling to say and never dare say something that they are unwilling to carry out: to say what one means and mean what one says—these reflexes must translate seamlessly, doubtlessly, and euphoniously as time becomes an ever-scarce luxury across sites of risk. This does not mean that criminal or violent sectors are not full of clandestine patterns (bluffing, camouflage): still, they never arise out of repressive weakness but rather as commissioned strategies. If called upon, one must prove the dexterity of ill intentions. For survival depends upon the decisive, immaculate capacity for synergism between mind, body, speech, desire, sensation, temper, movement, and will as a smoothly-turning wheel. Thus the war-poetess illustrates how a thin wire of atrocity can become a funnel, become propulsion, become storm and raid, until existential reality itself takes on the onus of the all-wronged.

Fifth Night (of the fatal lull)

Disturbances of the harmony among the elements can be of two kinds—natural or magical. Natural disturbances can result in one of four kinds of death. If, as the result of a wound, the body loses its blood, it is deprived of the element of water and the result is death. If we strangle someone by the throat or otherwise make breathing impossible, we've deprived him of the element of air, and he suffocates and dies. When a person freezes, he's been deprived of the element of fire. And if a person is dashed against some object, his solid matter is shattered and death is inevitable.

The magical causes of death, also referred to as medical, are far more intriguing. They are caused by the mysterious natural substances we call poisons. The object of natural science is to learn to recognize and also produce these substances. Every Ismaili can and should benefit from this knowledge...
Vladimir Bartol[52]

Can vile undertakings ever be conceived as demure? Can life-robbing sects be credited with weaving a delicate practice? To answer this question, we might revisit the ninth-century Arab polymath Ibn Wahshiyya, who deigned to write a Book of Poisons exploring all the careful effects of the slipped drink. This figure watched the slow or fast-acting properties through which organic tissues became mangled, warped, and irrecuperable (anthem: only the dead, only the dead). Alas, the coming centuries will also do business with these problematics of inhalation and ingestion (typologies of exposure) and their spectrum of powders, vapors, and elixirs.

The night-raid in an obvious sense is an attempt at a final overture: that of the last night, led by a recurrent force that stops other phenomena from returning. Let us call this the hour of the fatal lull, which requires in turn a philosophical definition of the ultimate. For what are the several standards through which we might designate something a limit-experience? What is the criterion of this ultimate?

See *complexity* [i.e., to prize sophisticated layers; to wind experiences like music boxes of the most elaborate compositions, as if filled with a thousand miniature gears].

See *immensity* [i.e., to trail events of expanse, as in natural disasters, where one measures earthquakes, hurricanes, or floods by the spatial scope of their wreckage and the amount of covered ground].

See *intensity* [i.e., to toy with heightened pulses, though this category breaks into many sub-compartments, for it is a different question to solicit the most vivifying type of infatuation as opposed to spite, frenzy, horror, agony, drunkenness, or rapture].

See *speed* [i.e., to reference those early shamans and futurists who praised acceleration above all else, trusting this concept alone to render things unstoppable and irreversible].

See *rarity, alterity* [i.e., to select based either on inimitability (the irreplaceable thing) or sheer transfigurative capacity — namely, mutational effect on whatever it carves against — which is most often upheld in groundbreaking technological sectors and the realm of disruptive inventions but also in the avant-garde's mad premium on originality. How unique, obscure, or innovative the vision and to what extent does it wrench perception away from normality and into altered states?].

See *"the last"* [i.e., to seek the final iteration of something— the once-and-for-all; the closing song; the midnight version].

Let us pause here to note our recurrent fascination in contemplating the last of a line, series, species, tradition, or fashion (the last gemstone, the last dynasty, the last human or architectural example of a school), for it harbors a subversive blow against both utopian and totalitarian ideologies. While utopian projects, even if they consider themselves the last system, always drape themselves in delusions of permanence (that the final society will hold redemptive durability), totalitarian projects similarly predicate themselves on assumptions of absolute supremacy. Hence to begin speculation of the last anything— hallmark of those mercenaries who literally dispense the last breath—is to entertain those sentiments of impermanence and vulnerability otherwise shunned by all civilizational regimes. Here we substitute the vigilante's organon for what is called reality, and with it the acquired taste of the night-raider: that there is nothing more beautiful than the person who is just about to lose a world.

The fatal lull requires one to imagine the night gone wrong, the loneliest night, and the night of the unfathomable materialized. What would you do if it were your last night on earth? This is always a rhetorical, frivolous prompt thrown around at dinner parties as a kind of time-passing entertainment, but to actually step into this question is a perilous, time-shortening task. It demands a certain sensitivity to whatever falls away and goes extinct, and to those creatures/substances that are somehow doomed.

Example: Vladimir Bartol (Slovenia, 1938). He decides to write a book about assassins, *Alamut*, and thereby reconjure the lavish fables of the *hashishin* garrisons ("those who smoke hashish") that wrought havoc upon the Persian Empire in the eleventh century. Alas, they are the most iconic representation of the term night-raider, flawless practitioners of the *shabi-khun* (blood-night), with the alleged words of their charismatic leader (the Old Man of the Mountain) — "All is illusion, thus all is permitted" — resounding in their ears. In the story, he is depicted correctly as an untrustworthy genius whisking individual minds into entranced obedience, and then sends them out as post-dusk squadrons like some pigeon-keeper on the roof who delights in watching his birds take flight (always gambling that these precious things might never make their way back). He flips the hidden switch of the uncommon in every setting and thereby establishes himself as the death-rattle for all that once was and all that has come before: such is the fatal reading of the ultimate as anti-destiny. Beware the one who trivializes Being: they are not to be trivialized in turn. He strolls through gardens, courtyards, minarets, and libraries; he surrounds himself with scrolls, potions, and exotic animal breeds; he teaches art, mysticism, and murder in the same breath; his decrees are unquestionable, though riddled with cryptographic turns. Indeed, his tongue feigns a sage-like ambiguity (that he merely advises), but it is an open-endedness that does not equivocate. Instead, every word is understood by the night-raiders as purest command, for his language carefully ratchets the listener (*ratchet*, meaning a bar-bearing mechanism with turning inclined teeth that controls steps or degrees, but also in continuum mechanics referring to a principle of accumulated plastic deformation, also known as "cyclic creep," caused by structural stress). He thus pressures gentle means into non-gentle ends with the serenity of the ultraist: another name for fatal lull. The Old Man perches, and they descend (as diffractional waves). This is how a short-lived clan becomes the subject of a tale that does not belong to any particular time, place, or genre: climax of the anti-climax; one book to end the everything.

Rest assured, the teachings of the night-raid hold across all spheres of futurity: they apply equally well to descriptions of both oncoming power formations and resistance movements; they are fitting hypothetical programs for the evolution or devolution of philosophy, literature, culture, and all aesthetics, or conceivably even methods of combating/expediting ecological or technological disaster. Here all become equal accomplices of a well-devised mood; here all throw dice in a cheaters' enclave based only on foul play. Is it so outlandish to hand the future over to the most sinister carriers of the will? Sometimes the fiend will save the world.

Chapter 4

Night and Secrecy

(Five Sects at the End of the World)

There is an old, frequently misplaced genre that perhaps, above all others, proves appropriate to the study of Night's relation to secrecy: The Book of Questions. From time to time, these elusive Books of Questions were found in certain mystical orders and monastic sanctuaries, their authors typically anonymous and having left nothing more than a series of ponderous hanging inquests to trouble the reader's mind into eternity. They did not attempt their own answers or interpretations, nor did they follow a consecutive line of argumentation: rather, one could conceivably open onto any page and sink into queries that ran aimlessly from one to another (stains of the inexplicable), noting that they also always seem to end abruptly (signaling death or madness without resolution).

The Book of Questions is therefore a seemingly evil, pathological, or at least apocryphal genre, for it does not alleviate but only compounds the daze of consciousness. And yet it reminds us of those mountain-climbers who at some point of desperation in losing their track, no longer able to distinguish the peak from the base or the way forward from the way backward, suddenly spot another hiker on route to the precipice. This approaching figure offers to aid them by guiding the rest of the trek, and accompanies the other's journey with confident strides; upon reaching the top, however, the first disoriented and exhausted climber looks back in awe to discover that the guide is no longer there. They did not cross paths with any real someone but rather hallucinated this figment in order to rescue themselves from certain death. The Book of Questions is no different: it is a roundabout mechanism of the life-saving psychosis. It is the fracturing of the one into a vital conspiracy of the many at the outer edge of despair.

So it is that we arrive at the central challenge of this chapter: to elaborate a philosophy of the secret society. And even more than this, to place ourselves in conversation with the practitioners of one that sought to be the last sect in existence (to complement the onset of the last world). Acéphale (literally "headless"); Paris, 1936-1939: a movement of acidic thought in a time of occupation and genocide that gathers in a grove behind a library on those nights when no one is watching. They bow before an oak tree once struck by lightning (a kind of ritual altar) and begin a hemorrhage of visions like none before or since. However, what is commonly overlooked for all their ravishing statements (tinged with bitterness and ecstasy) is an underlying theory of Night: for this nocturnality alone binds them to an atmosphere that makes possible the origin/end of a secret society. Thus, by extracting five distinct passages from five internal members of the sect, then situating these quotes like cuneiform script on the walls of a multidimensional shrine to the post-twilight, we will gradually perceive the inner workings of a clique whose night-oaths signified an experience of themselves as the last-of-us (without aftermath).

First Night (of the lightning)

On an area of marshy ground, in the middle of a forest where the reign of abandon and ruin is slowly being revealed, there stands a tree that has been struck by lightning. It is possible to recognize in this tree the silent presence of that which is expressed to us by the arms without a head of the Acéphale. We have the desire to seek out and encounter what men have always had the possibility of discovering, the vague presence that becomes the recognizable sign of the destiny of each of them. But this first attempted encounter on this night in the forest will only take place when death manifests itself there: to go in search of that presence is, as far as we are concerned, to seek to cast off the vestments that veil our own death.

Only night and silence were capable of giving a sacred character to the bond that unites us. As for the sulphur produced in the depths of the earth in which the roots of trees push downwards: volcanoes alone produce it, expressing for us the volcanic reality of the earth.

Georges Bataille[53]

Let us begin this chapter from a Book of Questions with a casual yet disturbing suggestion: Is Night itself the unspoken member or even leader of this secret society? Can we credit it as the driving force of mal-inspiration given the empirical possibility that none of these thoughts of the "sacred conspiracy" might have ever emerged except under cloak of the after-dark hours? Let us not underestimate the exceptional importance of the phenomenological detail of a "tree struck by lightning," for it implies that the entire theater of operation for this gathering was preceded by a nocturnal event of the nocturnal storm.

Extending this potentially instrumental role of weather and climatic sensoriality (think of the unique literatures developed by peoples living among locusts, floods, ice seasons, or stone avalanches), what do we make of this quote's reference to marshland that portends a topography of faulty ground? Do certain ideas derive particularly from the loss of sure footing and the experience of gradual sunkenness, leading us to a philosophy of the swamp, of quicksand, or of the bog? Is such unstoppable submergence yet another emblem of our being playthings in the hands of anonymous, inhuman forces (like being struck by the aforementioned lightning-bolt)?

Does Night also enhance the faculty of Pareidolia: i.e., the projection of an alternative meaning or image to a visual stimulus, like children who perceive animals in cloud-formations or faces on the moon's surface? The above-cited author mentions how the tree's presence holds some resemblance to their bizarre diagram of collective worship in the secret society of Acéphale, and so is this precisely the unleashing of that pareidoliac imagination which moves from vague shapes to distinct associations? Are the members of this faction deploying Night as a kind of projective test for themselves, like the Rorschach inkblot of the psychoanalysts or those mimetolithic patterns (shapes found in eroded rock strata) where ancient shamans believed themselves to sight the profiles of dead ancestors?

Does Night bear some connection to the hyper-consciousness of the abandoned or the abandoner, for we are told of a forest marked by the "reign of abandon," thereby leading us to a potential philosophy of the orphan, the defector, the deserter, the traitor, the hermit, the fugitive, or the wanted man? Does Night allow a sufficient breach—of separation, betrayal—from which thoughts of distance emerge in vivid capacity? This specialized vision of the faraway (rendered by some violence of the rift) is also perhaps the logic behind the terms "discovering" and "destiny" invoked above, each of which hovers over its own speculative valley. Nor is it coincidental that this abandonment-instinct is also often the preliminary formative gesture of the prophet who flees into the hills or caves to chase voices from otherworldly terrain, subject to the same hallucinatory effects of the Dark Room (prolonged isolation chambers or cellars) that mystics would enter to induce altered visionary states won only from the will to annihilation.

So it is that one key purpose of this secret society is said to revolve explicitly around death: namely, that they coalesce in a zone where "death manifests itself" and seek a type of nocturnal transparency (for "Night too is a sun," an elder reminded us) that sheds those oppressive "vestments that veil our own death." Does it mean that this grove is a kind of mirror-world or decadent looking-glass where they might stare at themselves in some uncanny skeletal form: to meet their dead or undead version? Is this shadow-figure (an encounter with that self lurking three steps ahead) hostile, vengeful, or delirious with anticipation? Is the secret society attempting to learn the difficult art of divination, which itself is tied to all the ornate rungs of the ladder of fatalism (missed fates, lost fates, obstructed fates, false fates, competing fates, illicit fates, hypothetical fates)? Is this an alternative orchestration of the so-called death-drive whose triumvirate included the simultaneous desire to die, the desire to kill, and the desire to become immortal? Or, is our secret society initiating itself via a desire to perish eternally and at the most intensified pinpoint of possibility, a cipher which this same author will trail forward when he writes of "the sounds of struggle lost in death like rivers in the sea, like the brilliance of stars in the night" and of a dying that "at once miraculously dazzled and transfigured"?[54] Perhaps the answer lies in the second half of that same verse wherein he alludes to "the unexpected," for is their quest one of reaching a terminal axis so singular, inimitable, and rare that it catches the entire world by surprise (philosophy of the pure ambush)?

Lastly, we arrive at a precarious recipe for those who would stray close to nocturnal energies: the sulfuric, the volcanic. Is our secret society following in the delicate footsteps of those early priestesses who practiced rituals at the mouths of live volcanoes? These women were not fooled by abstract theological principles but rather mesmerized by the iridescent color-schemes of the fire at night: this radiance alone is to what they devoted themselves and made sacrificial offerings. Elsewhere there is some further resonance in the author's statement that, "I imagine some female divinity dancing in the night, with a muffled violence, greedy for blood, mutilated bodies and death," though the night-dance here is complicated by the non-anthropomorphic inclusion of the universe as eruptive natural disaster.[55] For how does it drastically magnify or blur our cosmic lens when the overlord of Being is incarnated as a bubbling, scalding pit of lava and fumes? To kneel before fulmination? No longer transcendent or ethereally displaced in an above-soaring lair, nor even consigned to some mysterious underneath or nether-region of the afterlife, but rather pushing thought downward into the highly visible bottom of worlds (*le fond des mondes*). The temptation to fall, melt, or be swallowed whole in hot liquid pools? The crater; the fissure; the chasm of molten and vaporous release: what does it mean to wander across its ridge by nightfall, to study its angered profusions, and to emulate such examples of wrath?

Second Night (of the crucified)

This victim of torture, slumping under the golds of his halo, in the unreality of a night that weighs down on him without respite yet is heavy with promises of an unknown sweetness, offers himself, up, in his still-twitching perfection, like the brightly lit path along which rushes the sinner's heart, eager for its own interests. It is only through the Passion, whereby he seeks to take all horror upon himself, alone, that the ends offered to this heart arrive at a state of beatitude, but even so, in the moment of this death agony the relationship between sinner and God becomes confused with the one that is presented in the death on the cross, seen as an assumed existence, as a victim for all eternity.
Henri Dussat[56]

What is the function of this allegorical time-travel to the scene of an absolute crime (of the crucified one)? Why does this Night of the grand extinguishment, taking place over "long time" and in "empty space," give rise to what the author calls "new thirst?" What is to be gained from this lunar encounter with "the vanquished," "the damned," "the groaning one," and from our "lying broken at the feet of the corpse?"[57] Is it that the expiring messianic body is at once an orb (the fortune-teller's favored globular object) and an orbit (nexus of extravagant power)? This interception is rightly titled "Meditation before the Cross," for the careful choice of the word meditation ties us both to the *medium* (vessel) who reads the occult through cards, leaves, palms, scars, or from a thousand other inferential vantage-points, and also to its literal meaning of *meditate* as "to plan, rehearse, practice, study, and take appropriate measures" (the essential calculus of any conspiracy).

Many know that one rumored ambition of this secret society was to commit a human sacrifice, for which some allegedly volunteered to be killed but for which none wished to inhabit the hooded persona of the executioner. Was this meant as a parasitic enterprise (feeding off something greater than oneself) or a vampiric enterprise (feeding off something weaker than oneself)? Was it the banquet of the scavenger or the predator? Is it arranged to drain some affective nourishment from the lacerated form? Note, though, that the author does not follow the conventional temporality of the tale, for we are not stationed in Golgotha's hot daylight when the mobs throng to taunt the spectacle (repulsive beholding); instead, we meet the strung-up body at Night while it experiences radical aloneness (cold desert air, sounds of wolves). We are asked to picture it all again: the immaculate offering left squirming in discomfort along perpendicular wooden poles, the tear-stained face of the mother who watches helplessly against the ensuing wrong of ages, the absent father who commands the unbearable from his deterministic perch. But why would our secret society subject itself to this tribulation once more?

This visitation is not a symbolic witnessing but rather an energetic transference (less reminiscence than convulsion). It is the inhalation of the last breath of a murdered god in order to seal the transaction of blessing, curse, or altogether something else (vow, mission, haunting, revelation, possession). It is a cross-temporal circulation, bloodstream to bloodstream, nerve-ending to nerve-ending, whereby the wounded flesh of The Lamb, The Good Shepherd, The Prince of Peace, the Son of Man, and The Lord of Lords is re-vivified in the corpus of the secret society. Not the pristine affair of the resurrection but the more dirty business of necromancy. And the tragic irony in all of this? That conspiracy means in some sense "to breathe together," all the while crucifixion is a death by asphyxiation (eventually unable to raise the rib cages to allow the lungs' inflation). To become breath-taking thus requires a rendezvous with the suffocated.

The fact that the author uses the term "victim" rather than "martyr" attests to two essential qualifications about the massacre at hand: 1) that this vicious token is not an extension of some overarching moral consciousness, for victims are caught off-guard by sheer circumstance and hold no superior ethical imperative; 2) that this hanging figure has no instrumental connection to the future, for the victim does not unify the origin with the reckoning (it counts as no payment toward pre-emptive salvation) nor are they awarded some hallowed status of the new (whether that of the New Testament, the vanguard, or the avant-garde). We are not in the domains of necessity, covenant, or revolution. Instead, the descriptive indicators of "gold," "sweetness," and "the heart" render this a totally aesthetic event: the crucified is thrown there against the stake to secure "beatitude," a physical sign of grace or uplifting linked etymologically to beauty, thus explaining why no further standard biblical language is permitted beyond the term "Passion." Accordingly, it is quite consistent that, one evening in the grove, the secret society would ponder this single question: What color is the sacred? Not what does the sacred mean, nor how do we know the sacred, but rather its complexion, shade, and tincture above all else: to uphold the cataclysmic incident as something akin to a master's craft (artisanal whim or tinge). Is the secret society committed to subordinating all occasions to the rule of appearances; are they attempting to inhabit the principal structure of the guild?

The uneasy coupling of "still-twitching perfection" makes the crucified an exemplar of the torsion between pain and rapture. This also persists strongly in polytheistic cults who partake of drug paradises, most notably the *Aghoris*, those tantric Shaivites (devotees of the Hindu deity Shiva) of the left-hand path, who ingest *Aconitum ferox* (also known as "the long black sleep of night"). They smoke the dried roots in a practice that is part consciousness-expanding by entheogen (psychoactive substance that induces mood/perception alteration) and part ordeal-by-poison. They are also charnel-ground ascetics who dwell amid rotting fields and the open decomposition of corpses in order to attain *moksha* (spiritual liberation) in settings of great horror. They venerate deities of rage, and find in the fatal *Aconitum ferox* a drug that evokes extreme dysphoria (waking nightmares) in pursuit of the deeper euphoria that supposedly lies waiting on the other side. Is this the same paradigm with which we are confronted in the author's later piece in the secret society's compendium similarly titled "Meditation in the Forest," where the Acéphale adept describes a treacherous walking in the dark and the sensation of mortal endangerment by the elements as the group holds session in the woods? Is this the internal-nocturnal procedure of the one portrayed herein: "In the night of shadows and flames, that which has taken on the form of existence, in a being blessed with life, with human traits that are the same as my own, goes forth and beseeches death to appear to him in the guise of his own death."?[58] He talks of lanterns; he talks of insects; he talks of the misfortune of meeting his own image in this place, and of a vision of this half-laughing, half-crying double being torn asunder by a lightning burst to the chest. So it is that the expression *dead of night* returns to cold lips, perhaps always the best figurative encapsulation of this grisly causal dance between the ailing and the instantiation.[59]

Third Night (of the effigy)

> Another idol was the "Radiant," a stove adorned with the effigy of a woman who resembled the woman in a bust of the Republic. A true spirit of the hearth, enthroned in the dining-room, it was attractive because of the heat it gave out and the way its coals glowed, but was something to be feared because we knew, my brothers and I, that if we touched it we would burn ourselves. It was next to this stove that I was placed, having been carried down during the night when I woke up in the grip of fits of nervous coughing, which are the symptoms of "false croup" and which gave me the feeling—having been attacked by some supernatural evil of the night, ravaged by a cough that had entered me like a foreign body—that all at once I had become someone of importance, like a tragic hero, surrounded as I was by my parents' loving care and concern.
>
> Michel Leiris[60]

Is the first step in the formation of something as severe as a secret society the arrangement of certain toys in a little one's playroom? A startling choice of method: Why would the above author define sacred experience as the extraction of ambiguity (mist, marvel) from childhood objects strewn around the material home? This retro-anthropology (becoming smaller, younger) is neither a psychoanalytic regression nor a poetic nostalgia: instead, it is the restoration of a faculty to locate what is "at once attractive and dangerous, wondrous and cast aside...a combination of respect, desire, and terror."[61] It therefore comprises nothing less than a search for the right affective frequency of the effigy

71

(life-sized sculptural representation): not so much a substitute than an emanation that converts ordinary inorganic things into extraordinary animated beings.

The author begins by making inventories, listing those various decorative items around the house which emitted particular glowing potentialities (of trepidation, authority, escape). One of the first idolatrous examples, then, is that of the burning coal stove with a statue's head enthroned on top from which the child's imagination reaps two primary definitions: 1) that one must never get too close to the effigy, at once ever-present and yet primarily untouched in the architectonics of the sacred; 2) that its radiance must be feared, for it can harm or maim flesh through excessive proximity. Is this associative train of thought not identical to those narratives of mountain-prophets encountering God in alternative form (the burning bush), who must also take shape as wildfire (for the true body brings annihilation) and invoke a cryptic pseudonym of the "I Am Who I Am" (for the true name brings annihilation)? Presumably, this is done to diminish the inconsumable blast of its theo-presence, which leads us to ask: Is Night also of this quality? Is what we call darkness only a shrouded version of its actual conflagration, deflecting us from what is otherwise beyond endurance or comprehension?

The second detail to observe in the above passage is the recounting of a Night of affliction, an incident wherein the child is brought downstairs racked by sickness, fever, and hacking cough (always worse at night). The fact that he is positioned beside the idol-oven is not coincidental: rather, one must read it as a sign of election (the chosen) like those shamanic traditions for whom near-death experiences are signals that cruel forces of the universe have selected their future sorcerer. The child is thereby transfigured/elevated through suffering, though it is neither a random nor predestined practice that one be marked for dark communicative ability: these rare few are hand-picked only in times of looming threat. This prompts us to ask: What exactly must one become in moments of imminent collapse (extinction, disease, famine, natural disaster, mass lunacy), and must we read this outline of a child's perceptive reformation of the house as a practice of war-asceticism? Must we keep in mind that our secret society arose precisely at the witching hour of a war of the most grievous scale and typology?

The next descriptive passages of this piece speak to its very title—"The Sacred in Everyday Life"—for it prepares the scenic home's transition into a temple under siege. But as the daily goings-on start to morph and fortify space at will, one notes the consistent emphasis upon night-routines above all others, thus motivating us to question: Whose everydayness is so disproportionately night-bound? What absurd reconceptualization of banality entertains this gaze consumed only by the house in its after-dark stages? Two psychological pathologies come to mind that are predisposed to this forward-moving, precarious type of sight: 1) Hysteria, where certain subjects can experience exceeding delight in doubt (ambivalence, hesitation, vacillation, indecision, thinking twice) as a supreme pleasure-principle of second-guessing; 2) Cotard's Delusion (or walking corpse syndrome), where certain hypochondriac subjects believe that they are already dead, or have had their blood drained or organs stolen, caused by organic lesions or neural misfiring in the fusiform area of the brain, and often linked to Capgras Delusion's misrecognition of faces (such that one identifies both others and their own mirror reflection as impostors). Hence, our prescient question here is to ask whether Night (and its devoted secret orders) involves honing senses to mistrust the most fundamental assumption of the real: that anything is as it seems.

If we observe that the author conceives these nocturnal theories as a correspondence between his status in the secret society's forest grove and his recollections of strange contraband objects/practices in his childhood home, then we can conclude this Third Night study with the piece's focus on two separate precincts: the bathroom and the parents' bedroom. The first is a fascinating platform, for he describes locking himself with his older brother inside the lavatory and together devising narratives of remarkable adventure, intrigue, peril, sedition... "murders and kidnappings...the invention of war-machines, underground passages, traps and snares."[62] Some meet romantic or heroic ends, others are impaled in pits of spiked instruments, their fatalistic logic intentionally left opaque. Moreover, he depicts this nightly escapade of legend-making ("a secret mythology, which we resumed every evening") as a relation of initiates and neophytes in an underworld cult.[63] Thus we should clearly ask whether this category of magical power renders an invaluable beginning touchstone of the secret society: i.e., one that fuses pretending and pandemonium into a game of nightly storytelling? Must masters and disciples of the dark alike stay vigilant before processions of otherworldly motion within the uninspired—hence contesting the disenchanted shell of the prosaic?

Let us shift, then, to the second site mentioned above—that of the parental bedroom—which unlike the cavernous exoticism of the bathroom proves susceptible to a distinctly horrifying twist of the sacred Night:

There was my parents' bedroom, which took on its full meaning only at night, when my father and mother were sleeping there—with the door open, the better for them to watch over their offspring—and where I could vaguely make out, by the glow of the night-light, the great bed, the epitome of the nocturnal world of nightmares that prowl through our sleep and are like the dark counterparts of erotic dreams.[64]

The chamber of rest thereafter transpires as something beyond even the allusions to nightmare and eroticism (both of which still partake of an abstracted cleft between present and absent worlds). No, here we discover the most alarming trait of the child's imagination: to turn all human and non-human forms into effigies. All Being hereafter is mere gesticulation.

Indeed, does suspicion not become apotheosis in the wake of those hulking masses of the parents' sleeping bodies, as the staring child begins deducing that they are but iconic likenesses or facades possessed by some unnamed energy (the habitus turning inhabitus)? Is the trigger-point of a secret society this same night-drenched thought of abduction: that the living are but mere stand-ins or decoys of a subcutaneous existence that slinks beneath the narcotized surface of the everyday? Is what we call reality a simple morphine-drip (to subdue the pain of being worn like clothes) or lithium (to subdue the polar conflict of being maneuvered like dolls) that masks the fact that perhaps we do not belong to ourselves? What does it take to procure this malformed enlightenment of the marionette that turns everything foreign, inscrutable, cloak-and-dagger? Is the secret society's drawing of the headless figure—knife clutched in one hand, flaming heart in the other—the final exasperated affirmation that the house/night shudders at the manipulative behest of other fingertips? That the visible world is but a deceptive shawl for those who truly run the game? Is this not the very double-association of the word "outfit," which means both a secret ring of practitioners and a disguise?

Fourth Night (of the festival)

Simultaneously nightmare and paradise, the primordial age seems like the period or the state of creative vigour from which the present world escaped, with its vicissitudes of wear and tear and the threat of death. Consequently, it is by being reborn, by reinvigorating himself in this ever-present eternity, as in a fountain of youth with continuously running water, in which he has the chance to rejuvenate himself and to rediscover the plenitude and robustness of life, that the celebrant will be able to brave a new cycle of time. This is the function fulfilled by the festival.

Roger Caillois[65]

On the most select occasions, a Book of Questions would wager with a more futuristic voice, no longer contemplating universal or occluded subjects but those of the forthcoming world. This daring is what we seek here in the Fourth Night, though to trace this connection between nocturnality and futurity we must take an ironic detour to the primordial: more precisely, it is the ancient rite of the festival (explored by more than one author of our secret society) that must be plunged through futuristic tunnels of inquiry. Thus it is that we enter paradox, seeking the "fountain of youth's" secret of immortality from those who have been dead the longest and from an event recognized for its utter transience (a micro-verse that opens and closes for a single night, week, or month).

Does the secret society's rescued tale of the festival speak to our present's desperate need for a resurgent act? Are we standing at that epistemic threshold for which only the most originary mode of kinetic fervor and resuscitation can catapult us with the necessary traction to reach futurity? Is our arrival contingent upon this backtracking, meaning that we might otherwise not possess the fuel to get there? For each lesson that the festival teaches us, let us spin its foundational logic toward a futuristic paragon.

The opening paragraph of this Theory of the Festival is rife with the most powerful conceptual ingredients: descriptive experiential terms like exhilaration, conglomeration, contagion, exaltation, exhaustion, cheer, excess, and audacity tell the story of this pantheistic interval that enchants the city, village, or tribe beyond measure. Objects smeared with transgressive substances or behaviors marked by transgressive intent are no longer even perceived through the lens of violation (good and evil, purity and sin, sacred and profane, law and criminality). The festival is where bifurcations wither; the festival is the ecstasy of discordance.

First principle: The festival honors the divine ancestors. According to the secret society's author, these nights of paroxysm and metamorphosis are meant to relive a lost golden age wherein the ancients were capable of supernatural acts (impossibility) and enjoyed vistas of absolute richness (bounty). These heroic archetypes could fly stratospherically, teleport across space, move mountains with their brute force, transform into animals, or become invisible all the while feeding from generous lands free of famine, drought, disease, plague, or infant mortality. The opulence of the festival—its "spontaneous violence," the "promiscuity of the dance"—thereby reproduces the chaos of this bygone, exceptional paradise of the primordial ones.[66] Nevertheless, tribal legends then infer that the creation of the cosmos (or of the human race) somehow necessitated the imposition of certain limits, finitude, and laws of time, space, body, and being which led to the ancestors' extinction as well (this constraint represented doubly by the agonizing rites of fasting and silence that precede the festival's inception and also by the reclamation of social order afterward). Indeed, one must pay an entry fee of willed suffering for this ticket to the perfect-world show, and also must accept exile from the theater once the curtain closes. But what if instead of a re-enactment of the first days of the universe, the festival became something of a futuristic projection toward the last days of the universe? What if instead of worshiping the forebears, it became a tribute to the descendants? No longer the ceremonial glorification of the founder, the antecedent, or the progenitor but rather a recognition of the distant offshoot, scion, progeny, successor, or the unforeseen visitor who will undo our broken era? Not the one of lineal connection but the one approaching us with the total indifference and disconnect of estrangement? Counter-folkloric undercurrent (no nation, ethnos, or phylogenetic consistency; only inexistent categories): A festival for the arriving ghost of the stranger.

Second principle: The festival allows temporary role-switching. Masquerades, costumes, charades, pageants, veils, counterfeit: Actors are no longer discrete (individually separate) nor discreet (cautious, guarded); rather, they are entangled and flagrant amid unregulated pantomimes of otherness. The horoscopic characters and kinship-ties that usually dispense stratified fates now blend into an anarcho-scopic outpouring, and everything carried forward by the dominion of gestures (flailing, undulation, bowing, shrieking) over identity. The Night of Festival thus requires a philosophy of enticement to cross, commingle, and trade across existential lines. But what if this ephemeral game of reallocated lots did not have to culminate with a restoration to one's prior subjectivity? Can we imagine a future festival where one would not have to go back to the way things were before, but rather stay in the playacting stint of the meanwhile? To maintain the posture of the feigning one forever would make them the ideal Runaway—for we note the historical dilemma of the carnival or circus being that very few watchers ever actually ran away with the show, but rather only vicariously stooped beneath their decrepit tents for a spell. Or, at the very least can we foretell a Shapeshifter who follows but one rule: that no expended form, once indulged, can ever be resumed again? Like a game of cards where once a certain card is used, it becomes banned from play altogether? Does this self-dissolution and self-modification become easier in the futural streaming of the network (the profile, the avatar) as opposed to the older throes of the festival's orgy?

Third principle: The festival is predicated upon a

relinquishment of the taboo (forbidden practice or item). More precisely, the secret society depicts the "nocturnal debauchery" that takes place amid percussive rhythms and which ushers in such periods of cyclical defilement.[67] Still, while this elder hedonism always entails some element of the guarded (prohibitions that turn momentarily available), can we picture a futuristic night-festival wherein hedonistic experience is no longer designated at a certain time or with a scheduled closure? Does the futuristic ascent toward *instantaneity* make viable a spontaneous, fluid, or flash-like channel of desire where taboo circulates in constant aftershock and tremor? Moreover, would artificial intelligence transpose the carnal habits of eating, drinking, and singing into the domain of thought, making itself a hyper-stimulant accessible to mind-bodies that could trip with the single touch of a button or coding of a lone digit? What would ritualistic waste look like in the night of virtual consciousness?

[Side-Note: Archaeologists hypothesize that those Paleolithic groups who created the first cave paintings might have experienced hallucinations caused by oxygen deprivation (hypoxia) due to the enclosed atmospheres of the cave. Interestingly, those same conditions are sometimes known to occur for astronauts where states of altered consciousness, euphoria, and out-of-body sensations flare in the farther reaches of outer space. Would the future festival (perhaps ranging galaxies) also experiment with such cutoff respiratory flows?]

[Side-Note: Psychoanalysts around the same time as our secret society discovered that young children demonstrated problems in solving counter-factual syllogisms. Specifically, when confronted with a three-part logical sequence where the first sentence expressed an unrealistic premise—e.g., All wolves fly; Sebastian is a wolf; Does Sebastian fly?—the infants would object and cry out against the initial assumption that wolves are capable of flight (whereas older educated children easily recognized it as a test of abstract logic and thus overlook the irrational terms). Nevertheless, the most fascinating aspect of the research was that the young children would entertain the impractical or nonsensical dimension as long as it was introduced in a singsong voice or playful tone. Is this the same function as the festival, then? Does its musicality and frivolity guide revelers to be capable of accepting or even living by counter-factual syllogisms (to will the insurmountable)? In more futuristic terms, is all the rampant gamification that we are observing in almost all dimensions of the global order— disruptive technologies being marketed as games, social bonds turning into a form of online play, speculative economies and crypto-currencies that are based almost entirely on abstract numerical manipulations, and even politics resembling more a sports contest where pseudo-fanatical partisans cheer in the arena, going to lead to increasingly counter-factual exercises of logic? Can there be secret societies that hallow such nights of acute madness?]

[Side-Note: In the face of the author's continual emphasis on the primordial, we might ask what the future of secrecy itself might look like. Will there still be winding alleyways, secluded corners, or undergrounds to speak of, or any remaining tolerance for puzzles, riddles, rogue tongues, and mystification? In an age of constant surveillance and transparency, where each inkling, image, and impulse must be thrown into the spectacle of media, will there still be ways of carving out the subterranean dream of shadows? Darkness has often been synonymous with concepts of individuality, privacy, future, hiddenness, and freedom. In light of the incredible velocity at which the unknown becomes known in this age, eventually superseding even the speed of thought or light and snapping the neck of experiences into automatic déjà vu, what new formulations of the secret society will be conceived to contend with such accelerated realities? Will these groups partake increasingly of nether-informational technologies in a kind of digital Night? Will they form orders of hacker-monks in order to stay five steps ahead of the gauntlet? Will they protect the very possibility of the after-dark?]

Fourth principle: The festival is a recovery of the world's genesis story for the sake of rejuvenation. It is in this vein that the secret society's author declares that, "In every way, the primordial age must be actualized. The festival is chaos rediscovered and newly created."[68] He also observes that the dead are often allowed to trespass on the last night of the year as "ghosts, spectres, and phantoms are permitted to be rampant among the living."[69] But what if we tampered with the semiotics, optics, and symbologies of the festival to produce an end-world alternative (that of the pre-emptively exiting)? On the one hand, what if the future feast allowed no dialectical counterpart of a waiting base-reality but rather kept all participants in the grasp of devouring and simulation (or rather, of devouring the simulation itself)? On the other hand, what if the future festival was given an apocalyptic capacity (mal-singularity) that set fire to creation at its very collective climax? This final-night gala would thus have its own phantasmatic aspect, not linked to the dead ancestors but rather to the dying last specimen of the race not yet even born, envisioning their disappearance from afar or indeed becoming these languished ones ourselves if the festival could attain its wish of fatalistic proportions. [Note: A close associate (though no official member) of this secret society and elite philosopher of Night once spoke of his right hand taking on unstoppable momentum when he wrote, as if operating under its own independent volition, producing its own frightful content, and ultimately leaving him with just this one recourse: the left hand, whose only power was to stop the right hand. Can the future festival be conceived along the same axis, as a left-handed event that would stop the world from turning?].[70]

Fifth Night (of the return and the no return)

And this slow spider, which crawls in the moonlight, and this moonlight itself, and I and you in the gateway, whispering together, whispering of eternal things—must not all of us have been there before? And return and walk in that other lane, out there, before us, in that long dreadful lane—must we not eternally return?

Friedrich Nietzsche[71]

Sometimes the Books of Questions would trail off into ellipses, leaving a thought unspoken or unfinished in accordance with the Night's long-held pact with silence. Moreover, there is an elder here, one since vanished but occupying the forefront of the secret society's every move and inclination, a dreamer of the eternal return. This secret society did indeed return several times to the grove, but then eventually they stopped coming back. This is not the signature of their failure but rather their transportation into the debate of what another of the group would call "the vicious circle," a night when they find themselves "shattered there by the passage of time the destroyer."[72] Thus we conclude with the following conjecture: Could we fathom a Night that would simultaneously mark both the eternal return and the point of no return?

Part II

Four Interludes on Night

Alfred Kubin. "The Last King" (1902).

Interlude 1

The Mirror (Distortion)

(Original Text for Sacred Hill Video Essay, False Mirror Virtual Reality Project)

To enter a False Mirror is to risk watching ourselves distorted, transfigured, blurred, or irreversibly shattered. It is to sacrifice our own images to the virtual trickeries of its glass surface— where materiality and the ethereal, play and oblivion, bleed together seamlessly—though it holds all the dreams of the world. Still, one should be careful what one wishes for, especially when staring into false mirrors.

Sacred Hill

Sacred Hill is its own special dimension of the False Mirror, one of altered states found only at the limit of the body's disappearance. It is where we undergo the process of being consumed by a ritual machine, a contraption of mystical intensities that reaches deep into archaic spheres of occultism. Here all architectural laws are broken; here is where we observe the vanishing of identity and the enchantment of a stranded consciousness. For the Sacred Hill was created to take these four categories—tangibility and touch, transformation and time, vision and light, perception and perspective—to the edges of their excess, wonder, and disintegration. Here the soul itself becomes an object of pure imagination.

Calibration Room

All experiences of the outer boundaries are based on paradoxes, and so it is that we ascend a Sacred Hill by first descending, going far below, into a subterranean hall of ever-fragmenting mirrors that hide portals and gateways. This corridor leads us to a Calibration Room with a sort of technological altar at its center, the apparatus that runs our ritual, allowing us to initiate the first stages of entrancement: to make our bodies levitate, to abandon solidity and master the drift, while also reminding us of the price: that something must always be sacrificed to make the world sacred.

The first movement is to rise upward through fumes into a euphoric chamber; its formless, wine-colored walls remind us of those islands of the lotus-eaters where one becomes forever lost in ecstasy, forgetting how they ever arrived and never wanting to leave. Such is the first lesson of disembodiment, to endure the suspension of our very existence, and the first step into a circular labyrinth in which we will never be the same again.

This is also where we meet a mysterious figure: a fortune-teller, a reader of tarot cards, who selects one for us alone, hanging us in the balance of a single drawing, as if to tell us that fate is no simple game, and that futurity is always something of a perilous double-bind between will and chance. The card is therefore a riddle; its eeriness harbors the self that we do not recognize within us, like meeting someone in an alley who wears our face as their mask.

First Tunnel

Soon enough, we find ourselves in the first tunnel; its ritualistic conspiracy is unmistakable as we float through the ancient sacred design of the Ouroboros, that coiling snake devouring its own tail, its haunting image first found in the books of Cleopatra the Alchemist millennia ago, alongside the words "the all is one." The snake's intricate green scales start to constitute space itself, as we inhabit this twisted symbol of annihilation, resurgence, and eternity. More than this, it is here, in the radical strangeness of the first ring, that we gain a startling inhuman power: the ability to manipulate objects, to alter their trajectories and orbits through open air, with the simple motioning of our hands.

Second Tunnel

Still, some eternities last only an instant, and soon after we traverse into a second tunnel of hallucinatory contours. Here the surroundings pulsate and expand like a living organ or funhouse maze; we are in the delirium of the spiral now, the deranged blueprint of a mad architect who cannot tell the difference between high and low, beginning and end, narrowness and immensity. More than this, we are caught in an unstoppable carnivalesque rhythm, pulled through its passageway by an unknown gravitational force (something like a whirlpool). From the center of its spectacle, though, we learn the keystone of another power: that the cylinder's shape, time, and sound all swell or contract according to our own outstretched arms. Temporality bends to our fluid desire; movement surrenders itself to a dice-throw of our own choosing; the silhouettes and patterns around us are immediate extensions of our ability to accelerate, decelerate, or freeze time altogether.

Third Tunnel

The third tunnel envelops us in sudden darkness, like those medieval sages who spoke of searching endlessly within blindness. Thus we stumble through the pitch-black of a basement or the antechamber room of a ruined temple, all the while surrounded by esoteric diagrams inscribed on the stone walls, like those hieroglyphs of the great pyramids where the first sorcerers charted journeys of the dead. We face the cryptic logic of emblems and idols everywhere; they are written in tongues of the enigma, the rumor, and the whisper. This tells us that we are in the realm of absolute secrecy, where all the ciphers of the ritual coalesce, and where we must derive our third sacred power: that of illumination. Here our virtual hands become spotlights, able to trace the etchings carved across the ceilings and floors of this obscure place, each one a password or map into the otherworldly.

Fourth Tunnel

The fourth tunnel comes with a perspectival shift where we lose the ground beneath and subject our bodies to horizontal turning, for all destinies require some disorientation and vertigo, one that leaves us in perpetual freefall toward the Sacred Hill itself. Here at the final destination-point, tumbling down a cosmic balcony, we are given only partial and fast glimpses into the nature of the ritual itself: flashes of sacred geometry, mechanistic vessels, and vegetal landscapes all collide, bringing the pagan universe of primordial myths and the futuristic sectors of hacked perception into conspiracy together. So it is that the origin of all things and the end of the world might just be engraved in the same code, the same zone, after all.

Nevertheless, we are not allowed to linger in this atmosphere long, nor to inhale its metamorphic moods in large dosages, for soon two globes of black smoke appear: they follow us around; they threaten us ominously like playthings of the infinite, the impermanent, and the insubstantial. Their function is to enshroud us in a certain midnight, to bring about our gradual erasure and banishment from the Sacred Hill. Their hovering is no less than the sensation of the nothing itself, the breath and touch of the nothing upon our backs. So it is that all rituals end in a return...to the zero-degree (between shadow and silence).

(Original Text for Nerd_funk Art Installation Project)

Ray_oscopy (Post_Body)

They say that ancient mystics and schizophrenics often believe themselves to be shooting rays from their own bodies. These are where the religious visions of halos and also the paranoid sightings of alien ships beaming lights down to earth first emerge, in a delirium where one's own physical boundaries melt into trajectories of luminescence. Is this what is happening here? A kind of technically-induced radiation of solid forms into raining images, a looking-glass that converts flesh, bone, and blood into the sensorial wonderment of cascading screens. We are in an underground chasm where the walls are coated in animated organs and strange crystallizations; we are amid the pure excess of movements, shapes, and moods. This atmosphere is the very problem of the infinite itself: we are seeing too much, revealing too many dimensions at once; we are becoming vulnerable to the sheer derangement of omniscience, and the thin line between enlightenment and madness.

The confusing implications of the appendage are something that haunt us every time some new gloves, visors, or wires are strapped to the human hand, arm, head, or mind. We do not yet know the far-reaching implications of these supplemental limbs and lasers that extend as second skins. We might recall the initial history of armor and headdresses in tribal cultures, the first being an implement of war and the second of shamanic power. The sage's staff; the sorcerer's wand; the king's scepter; the priest's ring; the hypnotist's watch. Are we somehow throwing dice with the same equation: to adorn ourselves with magical effects?

Tech_Hole (Techno_Party)

This is the resurrected age of the festival, the bonfire, and the banquet. This is the new prototype of the masquerade, which first began the beautiful ritual of forgetting, dance, and the obliteration of self beneath the mask. It was in these halls of explosive consumption that humans first allowed themselves an escape from the prison-house of identity; here they could re-hallucinate reality; they could become twisted, malformed, enchanting, or iridescent. The blank domino; the wild card; the clean slate. Reset to the zero-degree in a whirlwind of colors, costumes, and choreographies. Thus, in this cylindrical zone we find ourselves carried into the excitation of a similar oblivion-sequence—videos, sound arrangements, half-forbidden stimuli on all sides that allow simulations to unlock ecstasy, laughter, raving, carelessness. This is where we come to lose the world.

The figure of the watcher is one that stretches across millennia. They are the living embodiment of an uncomfortable paradox: at once too close and yet cautiously distant; at once transfixed upon a certain object and yet never intervening; at once potentially heroic (as guardians) or disturbing (as voyeurs). The watcher must therefore master the technique of neutrality, anonymity, and disappearance; they must refine the art of synchronized rhythm and the balancing-act of seeing while going unseen. For this is the criterion of the perfect crime: to perceive everything while remaining forever imperceptible.

#N2 (New Nature)

Can the digital revolution offer us the aerial view of the gods? Does the algorithmic code alone possess the key to glimpsing creation through the lens of the universal and the particular? This means to exist in a state of full exposure to the wild; it means to inhale the air of the Open itself. Here we stare upon star-formations and geological patterns with the same gaze; we envelop both cosmological and terrestrial realms in a single stride; we suspend ourselves in outer and natural space with the awe of the traveler, the wanderer, the searcher. To tread into the drift of things means to enter all conceivable landscapes at once, and so here the seeker traverses forests, deserts, rugged and smooth terrain as part of the same quest. Except here they are not eternal settings; they are figments of the construct. The online archive is projected into the night sky, across horizons and along the world's surface, or even underwater, in order to manifest a new experience of the journey. This neo-nature has since become the debris of fantasy; it radically alters the meaning of the passenger, the vehicle, and the environment. We are in an ecology of illusory or hologramic planets, and read their signs like the pages of those old magical bestiaries with impossible creatures depicted behind every corner.

We used to envision the end-times coming at the hands of divine wrath (judgment) or elemental fury (disaster): such nightmares took the form of plagues, floods, flames, earthquakes, ice ages, or storms. But currently we dream only of technical catastrophes lying in wait: to understand this radical shift, we must descend the spiral staircase into the laboratory; we must sit once again in the domain of the mad scientist and make inventories of marvelous, disruptive invention; we must entertain the evil or accursed energy of the device, the apparatus, the button, the blueprint, and the project. Are we not mesmerized by the thing that could spell the end of all things?

#Mortal_7 (Cyber_Identity)

There has always been a simultaneous fascination and terror of the shadow; it somehow both enhances and threatens the mortal figure. We are never quite sure what it wants from us, why it follows us everywhere, why it unveils our internal nothingness in a vague and formless obscurity of the silhouette. We suspect that the shadow might even hold a separate destiny than ourselves, or that it might someday overthrow our human throne. The primordial fear of this lingering outline, however, is only magnified by the advancements of our hyperreality. Now the dark double takes on new names: the clone, the cyborg, the replicant, the avatar. A host of walking, breathing, ominous simulacra—endlessly reproducible and exponentially cunning in their artificial intelligence, and holding the one most desired gift sought by humans since the inception of consciousness: immortality. Do we need a new race of storytellers to tell the tale of these undying cyber-identities? Here we look upon them in their multi-dimensionality and apocalyptic potential. Each of these synthetic personae are ready to be awakened, vivified, and tempted forward, to become angel or monster at our single touch, though all the while we retain a one last power over these bloodless machinic abstractions: the power of finality, to end and undo them, the doomsday breath: to whisper them into vanishing.

Have we trespassed into the altar of some unknown temple? They are fast asleep in hyperbaric chambers, or perhaps they are the virtual equivalent of coffins. Do we wish them to slowly open their eyes and recognize our presence; will they behold us as ancestors or enemies? We might ask them to be gentle, even if they have come to challenge our territorial dominion over this existence; we might warn them that they have been born in order to manifest the great test: that is, to see whether the unexpected, fabricated being can actually surpass the so-called authentic forerunners of the game. Has this dangerous temple always been resting behind some invisible curtain, and ourselves always meant to serve as sacrifice?

#Sub_Terranea (Augmented_City)

The cityscape: mirror reflection of modernity's thirst for expansion, acceleration, and layered chaos within order. But now we take this urban immensity, this insane centrifuge of streets and alleyways, to greater acidic levels: Behind the wheel of a phantom-car that circulates at warp speed, we plunge through a labyrinth for which there is no longer any concept of beginning or end, truth or lie, origin or destination. Is it a path or a freefall? Is the winding augmented city of cement and neon billboards a false paradise of distractions and lost time? There are no dead-ends here, only the inexorable kinetic force of a vessel reeling toward futurity or absolute nothingness.

There are bad types in the hidden corners of this place; the wasted ones; the forked tongues; the discarded, soulless agents of its coldness—those with nothing to lose in their encounters:

the marauder, the opportunist, the thief, the predator. They view everyone as mere strangers; no intimacy, no shared fate; all are outside their inner circle, and all must pay a price for crossing here. They are at once seductive and deviant; they mix innocence and guilt, decadent play and malice, in the same cruel skillset. To survive them, one must accept and intensify the intruder's own elusive logic: quicker, more cunning, more merciless than any others of this dystopia. To become the worst imaginable actor of the cityscape: it may be the only way out.

Interlude 2

The Fire (Restraint)

(Interview with Dana Dawud titled "Restraint: Between Fire and the Labyrinth"
"The Derivative": Issue 12/01/2020)

Restraint (another nocturnal password): For we must be careful what we say at night; we must be careful who we meet and what streets we take at night. To tread cautiously, if ever to exit in one piece: for there is everything to lose on the night-gone-astray.

Dana Dawud (DD): The deadlock of theory of a kind which calls for a totalizable understanding of political or economic systems is that it usually starts with wrong premises and ends nowhere. Envisioning future economies based on dualities such as need against desire requires that we do away with the actual multiplicities of economies which exceed our desires and needs. There are war economies, shadow economies, collapsed economies, distributed in manners that are heterogeneous and mediated by breaks, surges, and ruptures.

At this juncture in time, we are faced by this intellectual and spiritual restraint: "Where is the road to the road?" In your book *Omnicide*, one of the numerous labyrinths you construct begins with lines from a poem by Mahmoud Darwish: "My heart exceeding my need, hesitant between two doors/ entry a joke, and exit a labyrinth." What does it mean to exit a labyrinth?

Jason Bahbak Mohaghegh (JBM): Let us begin from the most malevolent element of this premise: that to awaken in a labyrinth means to exist in someone else's architecture, and thus to be the plaything of preconfigured disadvantages (designed against its inhabitant). Unlike the figure of the game-master, the riddler, or the puzzle-maker who actually hope that their clients overcome the elaborate challenge, instead we picture the delight of an overseer who deploys complexity solely for the sake of condemnation and spectacles of futile wandering. Their wish is either to eternally elongate the failure or to have you die there (amid surrender, brokenness, exhaustion).

1. The first strategic impulse to surviving the labyrinth is therefore restraint: more specifically, to restrain oneself from the very desire to move and thereby disabuse the panicked reaction toward flight/searching/escape. Instead, one must resist falling further into the labyrinth's logic of entrapment (where every step sinks irrevocably) and entertain the possibility of the no exit, no beyond, no way out. We learn this lesson from the Minotaur—perfect embodiment of austerity: no friends, no furniture, no titles or decorative embellishments of the atmosphere—who attunes himself to the bareness of flesh and stone alone. This restraint (forfeiting all dreams of the outside) is a fatal affirmation: it gives him absolute dominion over all who enter; it endows him with a rare, lethal focus combining animal instinct with monstrous consciousness.

2. Secondly, we must consider the backdoor relation between restraint and effusion as a tactic of labyrinthine quality. If one studies the ancient rituals of banquets, festivals, or even grand cannibalistic celebrations (indulgence, excess), one notes that the devouring hour is most often preceded by long bouts of fasting (deprivation). The pendulum therefore swings between the starved and the explosive, just like the containment of water or air generates the event of cloudbursts.

To this same end, there is indeed a secret embedded in the depictions of the tranquil warrior in ancient narrative traditions, for these epics often imagine the fighter roaming along desolate beaches or dwelling alone for years in mountain castles. These images of prolonged idleness always precipitate the later rage that shakes universes upon the warrior's re-emergence. This is not a theory of conservation of energy but rather the accumulation of energetic potential (the hoarding, stacking, and then projection of temperamental intensity), for as one obscure artist once said: "Only density does not lie." Moreover, it also links restraint to the notion of biding one's time: in effect, sitting out certain rounds and waiting for the opportune moment to leap/strike (excellence in both wrath and craft). This is not a philosophy of passivity, then, but rather a philosophy of maximized chance.

3. Thirdly, let us follow those ascetic figures (monks, mystics, martial artists) into the far distances where they took vows of silence, poverty, flagellation, or degradation as routes to divine ecstasy. Let this be understood: that the most incendiary versions of this practice had nothing to do with piety, modesty, or transcendent worship but rather constituted wilder gambles toward the pure windfall of a becoming-god. Hence such agonizing codes of restraint (mutilation, hunger, solitude, filth) were nothing less than lottery bets whose stakes reached toward the ultimate turn of fortune: apotheosis.

With these initial trajectories established, I would add only this final note: that restraint can in various circumstances exercise a profoundly subversive quality in that it stops a repetitive world. More exactly, it halts the tyranny of the same by discontinuing habit (myths of identity fall apart), succession (myths of power fall apart), causality (myths of reality fall apart). Thus we return to those same mystics cited above whose radicalism lay not in direct confrontations but rather in the gesture of walking away from the world. Stated otherwise, sometimes to leave the labyrinth one must first abandon/forget the very notion of the labyrinth itself (this oblivion is its own willed restraint).

[Note for later: Revolutionary regimes are always faced with a question (upon assuming control) of whether to gratify their right to bloodbath, purging, and political vengeance against former enemies or whether to practice restraint. For what are the high costs of consecrating a new era amid executions and mass graves? A typology of aftermath that risks playing with cyclical fire.]

DD: The trajectories you map to obliterate the tyranny of the labyrinth signal timescapes, temporalities mediating the dense stacking of potentialities and the radical throw into chance... What shapes do these temporalities take and how can a philosophy of chance be understood, are they somewhere other which keeps spiraling into virtual eternal moments of possibility or are they a parade of presents which push us further into futurity?

JBM: This question dares us to describe various philosophies of "restrained time," and to ask paradoxically how certain practices of binding, coalescence, and tightening (criterion of the spell) might open secret temporalities. For the first gate to any secrecy is always a vow of restraint.

Let us start, then, by imagining five unique powers held over time and alongside them five particular practitioners of these abilities: 1) the one who echoes time; 2) the one who freezes time; 3) the one who ricochets time; 4) the one who carves extra slits within time; 5) the one who surprises time (with untimeliness). No doubt, each figure must restrain some component of experience in order to gain such exceptional techniques, just as martyrs die young in order to access a certain alternative immortality, wielding existential contraction in a way that allows them to play the long game of the eternal. Thus we ask again: What must one first acquiesce (the restraining price) in order to manipulate each of those concealed temporalities noted above?

To speak of the echo is to engage a timescape of partial resonances, most of which arrive too late and with lost origins. To speak of the frozen is to engage a timescape of suspended animation, where the clock's slender hands ice over and phenomena mimic states of pure standstill. To speak of the ricochet is to engage a timescape of elastic collision, to subordinate all trajectories to the detour and the deflection, to the supremacy of the angle, as everything moves according to its own chaotic geometry. To speak of the carving is to engage a timescape of miniscule incisions, those that extend events by split seconds and thereby purchase a single stolen breath more in every transpiring instant. And finally, to speak of the untimely is to engage a timescape of irrelevant infiltrations and ambushes, where those deserters who willed themselves posthumously ("only the day after tomorrow belongs to me," he says) punish each self-important moment with tremors of the unexpected, the unparalleled, and the no-right-to-have-been.

But now let us wrest these five schools of restrained time from abstraction and unravel them across a visceral axis known both to the darkest totalitarian settings (the prison) and to the collapsing worlds of failed states (the riot). What do each have to offer those despairing in dank cells or those flung amid debris? What force of consolation do secret temporalities render to the equally horizonless destinies of the tortured, the ruined, and the displaced? We can imagine the echo as something that smuggles messages into and out of the room of solitary confinement; the frozen as that which allows a captured final glance of a society burning down; the ricochet as a means of turning brutal impacts elsewhere and wherever (nihilistic wish for the anywhere but here); the carving as a narrow window to savor, mourn, or curse the passing world-under siege; and the untimely as a vision (what saves nothing, redeems no one) that nevertheless accounts for those conceivable unborn worlds that pile up in archives of the hypothetical. For they also have their reckoning, in some silent eventuality.

Hence, it is no coincidence that three of the most iconic authors of the Arab world, all simultaneously withstanding the Lebanese Civil War from their different vantages in the heart of Beirut, would compose silhouettes of the damaged city that experiment with such strains of time-disturbance. Mahmoud Darwish writes: "Three o'clock. Daybreak riding on fire. A nightmare coming from the sea. Roosters made of metal. Smoke. Metal preparing a feast for metal the master, and a dawn that flares up in all the senses before it breaks." Ghada Samman writes: "When dawn broke, we were all staring at each other in amazement, wondering: How did we stay alive? How did we survive that night?" Adonis writes: "Through the years of the civil war, especially during the siege, I learned to create an intimate relationship with darkness, and I began to live in another light that does not come from electricity, or butane, or kerosene. / This darkness, this secret light, can wrench you even from your shadow and can toss you into a focal point of luminous explosion." Prophets of high restraint, overlooking the touch of catastrophic centuries with a consciousness somehow not of this age: We play eavesdropper to their disquieted words in order to trace the footsteps of such shadow-temporalities.

All of these tactics hold crucial applications in the most devastated places, whether in the dungeon or the street. And all of these demand a dire tradeoff of some kind from their subjects, for most often secret temporalities are won by selling away our remaining shares of linear time. Such is the inexorable war between the chronological and our best dreams of delirium/flight, and a reminder that "endurance" (perhaps the most vital concept we can fathom) is itself also a principle of restraint.

DD: The temporality of restraint is one of sacrifice and endurance, sacrifice as an active force of creation, offering arising subjectivities forms of control over their dwindling fall. Artaud writes: "I no longer wish to be possessed by Illusions./ I have had enough of this lunar movement/ making me name what I refuse and refuse what I have named. I must end it. I will fall into the Void." It is this break with linear temporality and teleological representation that allows the different forces and tactics you have previously outlined to be traversed. In the same text Artaud speaks of fire.

Fire has been a recurring motif in my readings this year, it's as if I keep seeing it everywhere I go, in books, images, and real-life events. There is something about fire which always creates a break in how layers of life are perceived. In Kleist's novel *Michael Kohlhaas*, the protagonist, faced by injustice, sets everything in his sight into raging fires, once fire is introduced in the novel, it engulfs everything, it even takes the place of metaphors and descriptions of affect and emotions of different characters. Everyone speaks the language of fire. Kohlhaas encounters a gypsy woman who is known for her prophecies, she turns her gaze upon him and gives him a paper, and tells him it would save his life. When he is caught and is sentenced to execution, right before being beheaded, he swallows the paper and the secret within it. What could fire tell us about restraint?

JBM: This is a beautiful last move to the dance (note: choreography itself is almost always about negotiating the secret pact between restraint and movement). Consequently, your overture here requires us to keep company with the ancient fire-worshipers whose priests of the eternal flame would stand guard all night in the temples to prevent its extinguishing (sacred insomnia as restraint); or to sit in the caravans of old fortune-tellers who offered themselves as vessels of fatalistic bursts, reading incendiary particles of messages encapsulated in their crystal balls or in scattered ashes (oracular inspiration as restraint); or to study with the first pyrotechnic guilds who discovered the capacities of self-contained exothermic chemical reactions, and whose fireworks displays were semi-miraculous manipulations of heat and light (spectacular detonation as restraint). All of these various alliances realized that the setting of great fuses in the world requires patience, neutrality, pressure, and the allowance of a countdown. All of them knew that their likelihood of stealing powers from the infinite (like any Promethean theft) depended entirely on the minimalism of their gestures—subtlety, slightness, anonymity, and the will to imperceptible violations.

For one is careful when playing with fire.

Interlude 3

The Fallen (Savage)

Those savages of whom it is recounted that they have no other longing than to die, or rather, they no longer have even that longing, but death has a longing for them, and they abandon themselves to it, or rather, they do not even abandon themselves, but fall into the sand on the shore and never get up again—those savages I much resemble, and indeed I have fellow clansmen round about, but the confusion in these territories is so great, the tumult is like waves rising and falling by day and by night, and the brothers let themselves be borne upon it.

Franz Kafka, "The Savages"[73]

Three footsteps into an abyss and already we encounter three different terminologies for the same group: the savages, the clansmen, and the brothers. Does this triumvirate of names represent a gradual transfiguration or sequence of ritual phases? Do these pseudonyms imply that they walk along three vital axes or descend across three deadly staircases? Should we worry that this sliding scale from formality to intimacy— savage, clansman, brother—will somehow heighten the risk of our trespass into this realm of the doomed shoreline and make all thoughts of return/reversal impossible?

No doubt, it seems that we are confronting nothing less than a secret society of the abyss, which necessarily places us in the logic of exclusion, ambush, and covert war. But who are these strange practitioners of the surrender (falling to the sands), and what obscure logic of semblance and resemblance binds them together as they wash away beneath the tidal foam? The narrator begins from a voice of almost anthropological distance and neutrality, using the classical designation of "savage" to describe an unformed world-view presumably in opposition to the complex thought-formations of the passage itself.[74] Moreover, the intricate depiction of their gesture cannot help but stutter and turn on itself ("or rather, or rather"), at first simulating a nervous series of clarifications that we later learn might actually be the sound of a trap's many bolts locking around us. There is no anxiety here: they have played this game before; they know exactly what they are doing.

The second classification—"clansmen"—only further maintains this circle's anonymity while also signaling an alliance that follows the predatory or hunting paradigms of early tribes. The abyss is therefore precisely where we meet the radical foreigners or cut-throats with zero loyalty to our ways; our despair brings no mercy, as we find ourselves chased by those whose apparent coldness is its own delirium (that has nothing to do with us). Let us note the absolute calmness in this realization that their dream is our nightmare.

But the third honorary title, above all others, is the stuff of bad omens. "The brothers," he whispers in a way that chills any reader's spine, for it means that they have forged some other continuity down there in the chasm, one for which salt water functions in the place of bloodlines and generational inheritances are inscribed on pitch-black waves. There is no indication that they are sacrificial offerings, for if anything their silent bodies serve as anti-messianic warnings. It is conceivable that they have lived for eternities in this half-space of darkness, and it is also conceivable that the technique of increasing proximity to the ocean's border—becoming brothers precisely at the moment they cast into its rolling depths—tells us the perspective of the actual narrator behind this fragment (what unites the liquid, the horizon, and the bottom).

There are only three contingents that would experience closeness to those abandoned rhythmically to the "rising and falling by day and by night": the drowned, the lost-at-sea, or the sea itself. Thus, we are compelled to wonder whether we are being stalked/enveloped by ghosts (those with unfinished business among the living), deserters/runaways (those who have mastered the art of disappearance), or by the patron god of this island nowhere itself (that oceanic consciousness which houses the malice, void, and restlessness of the sunken).

Interlude 4

The Pretender (Future)

We are going to speak of the future. Yet isn't discoursing about future events a rather inappropriate occupation for those who are lost in the transience of the here and now? Indeed, to seek out our great-great-grandsons' problems when we cannot really cope with the overload generated by our own looks like a scholasticism of the most ridiculous kind.

Stanislaw Lem[75]

The Pretender is both the protector and harbinger of Night's interface with futurity. So it is that one can extract three minimalist passwords only delicately evident in the texts of Stanislaw Lem's *Summa Technologiae* that might assist in sketching this formulation: those of the pythonic, the enigmatic, and the monstrous.

Pythonic—The first minor motif taken from beneath the dominant waves of such writings is a grappling with an age of sheer pythonic stature, but intriguingly not only the immensity of manifesting technologies and excessive ideas, but also the immensity of lost things, vanished eras and forms, unanswered questions, and even more ominously the immensity of unrealizable projects. After all, the term vast comes from the Latin *vastus*, meaning huge void/emptiness, which also then becomes linked to the term *devastation*.

If one reads *Summa Technologiae* closely, there is often an undercurrent of sorrow over the inevitable waste that the author foresees at every twist of the future: particularly, the more he talks about the exponential growth, amplification, and accumulative momentum of scientific problems, he goes back to this perpetual concern that there are not enough human beings on earth to walk all of these trajectories to their limits. This raises the question: What won't we get to in time? So our own physical finitude is the enemy of our scientific imagination and horizon of discovery (he says that some fields unavoidably will have to be cut, some problems will be neglected—which leaves us stranded in minefields of suspicion and doubt over the untested zones). In this outlook, history itself starts to resemble a role-player video game where one acquires objects along the way not knowing their use-value or appropriate context until much later, sometimes by the time of their impracticality or obsolescence. Or, like a "choose your own adventure" story where the reader sits in extreme tension over the fact that they always have a recursive view of time that circles back to either validate past decisions or shows them to be fatal flaws—did you go left or right; did you go into the forest or into the castle; and often you have no immediate criterion by which to judge what will save you or kill you. And this has always been an existential problem not often talked about in philosophy—how does one grieve for the hypothetical self or hypothetical reality that never even emerged because you chose willfully to ignore it in pursuit of another? How do we engage those immaterial worlds that were given no chance to crystallize? How do we mourn lost destinies, because to select one fate always also means to ignore or banish every other potential fate that could have surfaced but instead remained in the swamplands of abstraction? And we actually have a term for this emotion, on those rare occasions when we experience this haunting or strangled echo of the "what-could-have-been"—we call it "Regret." And so this leads back to our first question (since later the same text will allude to phantoms, who by definition are precisely figures of unfinished business, poor choices, and violent resentment): Is there a way of knowing what we will inescapably regret in the beyond?

Enigmatic — The second fascinating thematic, and it is a subtle one in these chapters, is that Lem almost borders on affirming a long-held mystical notion regarding the enigmatic nature of truth. He does this in his assault against certain types of induction and his privileging of others, where he seemingly suggests that we need to start looking at the future as a convoluted, emergent property. Recently some intellectual figures have been returning to this premise and fashioning it as a novel insight, but one can find its traces permeating the writings of the Sufi dervishes and Shaolin monks and the cosmologies of indigenous tribes along with even the more heretical writings of Christian monastic figures: namely, that Being itself is cryptic. That's partly the etymological intent of the word Zero in English, which comes from the Arabic *sifr*, forming both our later words zero and cipher, because the origin of all things is a puzzle.

In any event, this inverse logic of enigma blames the world itself for its perpetual foreignness — since in philosophy and science often the presumption is that truth itself is perfect, immutable, pristine, and that it's only a problem of our own flawed and partial perception that misunderstands truth and relegates it to obscurity, blurring, or occlusion. In effect, we catch only partial glimpses not because truth itself is confusing, but because *we* are confused. But what if this is wrong? What if so-called truth itself, or Being, or World, or Reality is itself intrinsically amorphous or elusive? Then we are in the architecture of the labyrinth, where the deeper one treads the more one's movements become a lost cause of futility, and this is how *Summa Technologiae*'s argument in suchchapters is structured: that every turn leads to three further doors (which is to say a multiplication of tangible unknowns).

Now let us say this is correct: that we are dealing with a nebulous concept of creation. My question (and it is the logical subsequent question of this work) is the following: Is there a way of adapting consciousness to volatility, irregularity, distortion? Avant-garde aesthetics and theoretical physics have tried to meet this challenge somewhat in the twentieth century, from cubism to splatter-paint to parallel universe theories— each school deploying their sensitivities toward unstable, disproportionate, decentralized, and bizarre reams of possibility. And their instincts were prescient, since the more technology allows us to explore macro and micro levels of existence, cosmic and molecular, the more we perceive it as a chaos scaffolding. But again, are there ways of adjusting consciousness to better engage such evasive, mist-like phenomena?

Sometimes one must leave realms of contemplative luxury (which philosophy, art, and science can all fall into) and follow figures who are the actual practitioners of a thought: What is the criterion of a practitioner here when we are talking about turbulent, frenzied, or erratic forces? 1) Those whose bodies and sensorial existence are viscerally dependent on the practice (so they eat, gesture, or survive based on it); 2) Those who treat these disturbing, insoluble movements as a craft (which means being led by a sense of urgency to devise things, turning anarchy into an apparatus or machination); 3) Those who engage these questions with mortal danger (meaning that getting the modality right is a matter of life and death). So I can give you three tangible examples: 1) Professional gamblers who endure marathons of insomniac time at the casino tables just to learn the choreographies of chance, for any professional gambler will tell that after a long while of studying probability and more importantly luck (which are not the same things; they are stepsisters of a certain kind but not identical at all), one starts to develop a sixth sense or instantaneous sensitivity toward the way dice or cards fluctuate; they can read strange, vague intensities behind these emblems of fortune, which is why they are exceptionally precise figures but also extremely superstitious (the same with athletes—they practice systematically with militant diligence for hours every day, but they also abide by superstitious rituals, and we should not dismiss this as mere unreason or nonsense but rather as an alternative typology of sense altogether); 2) Beyond gamblers, there is also a long wondrous history of martial arts masters of early Kung Fu who learned how to fight while drunk or to fight during storms or at high altitudes where the air was thin and vertigo was ever-present, just like guerrilla and tribal warriors for millennia have trained themselves to fight in the uncertain terrain of forests, mountains, jungles, or the sliding sands of the desert; there are also certain forms of sword fighting from the medieval era which are developed especially for rocky hills or ridges or dueling on staircases where one's vertical status is continually shifting; 3) And finally, even pirate culture has writings instructing crew members on how best to load gunpowder into cannons while experiencing the undulation of the ocean waves or firing in the dark; and they practiced this and ran drills while out on the sea and during the worst tidal gravitational pulls to achieve this need for navigating the unruly. And the secret here, by the way, is that the conceptual keyword of all of them — gamblers, martial artists, tribal or guerilla warriors, pirate factions — is not "control" but "vulnerability." They expose themselves to backbreaking degrees of vulnerability.

So yes, there are ways of aligning intuition, perception, sensation, and the speculative mind toward these territories of confusion, imbalance, optical illusion, and sensory disquiet. For that, though, we must deviate from quests for the absolute or the perfect and instead willingly enter fever-dream states, and to grasp whether there are refined ways of dabbling with moods, whims, or spontaneous occurrences. And for those who would ask how this concept could apply to something like science, one might be reminded that the foremost literary depictions of doctors at the outset of western modernity, Dr Faust, Dr Frankenstein, and Dr Jekyll (who becomes Mr Hyde), are all lunatics. So visionary science was allied with insanity (or more specifically mania and delirium) in the view of those who started this runaway train of modern technological advancement. And one should also recollect that those schools of scientific thought which presumed to operate according to rational structures (of determinism, causality, universal axioms) gave rise to some of the most bizarre experimental methods of all time. Just look at the origins of psychoanalysis itself: in the search for the supposed foundational, underlying code of psychic experience, what do these serious men and women of science resort to as the earliest legitimate instruments of analysis? Inkblots, hypnosis, cocaine, electro-convulsive therapy, bioenergetic analysis, and staged photographs of hysterical women writhing on asylum beds.

Monstrous: The third and final element to note sprinkled lightly throughout *Summa Technologiae* is its references to monstrosity. One section of the third chapter is titled "Ghost in the Machine"; then we have an entire chapter titled "Phantomology," but notice the small digression in which Lem alludes to the weird ancient paradigm of the Homunculus: which is an unnaturally created small semi-human being, usually by occult means, often linked in folklore and theology to evil and vampirism, and in alchemical circles to the goal of artificial regeneration. Thus he writes the following: "Cybernetics today is haunted by the medieval myth of the Homunculus, an artificially created intelligent being."[76] And elsewhere he uses the old Jewish term Golem (meaning a perverse animated creature made of inanimate matter) as the title of one of his essays about supercomputers.

Still, Lem might not be aware of the original definition of the Homunculus according to early alchemist orders, which is far scarier—according to the Egyptian Zosimos of the third century AD, one of the first recorded quotes on the Homunculus happens when he says that he himself actually met a priest who could turn "into the opposite of himself, into a mutilated anthroparion" (*anthroparion* here meaning a tiny, deranged version of oneself). Now, we could conjecture for several nights on what this forewarns: Does this Homunculus of the modern age, which could be artificial intelligence or the clone or the cyborg, also mean a mutilated inversion of ourselves? Is it something like the psychoanalytic double, which is an uncanny remnant of the Mirror Stage when we first become fragmented, incomplete, and traumatically alienated from ourselves? And yes, it does remain a question whether the digital screen (or the black mirror) indeed has a similar thieving effect as the psychoanalyst's mirror (robbing us from ourselves)? Furthermore, is this technological Homunculus the path to our immortality, or is it an enemy or death-wish or curse, or is it paradoxically both, which is the basic paradox of most monsters: that they have accursed immortality? And something brilliant mentioned quickly, despite having dire consequences, is the notion of the trade-off again: namely, what needs to be violated or sacrificed or killed in our originary forms in order to win passage to the next level of the Homunculus. Paracelsus, who is a later medieval figure (and the "father of toxicology") that also makes reference to the Homunculus, claims that the condition of its survival is that it has to be "nourished in a horse's womb for forty weeks with human blood." So what intimate dimension of self has to be offered as a token or tribute to the newcomer or fiend? *Summa Technologiae* opens these ontological questions by referring to monstrous names here and there, and we know that monstrosity often simply embodies the human experience itself taken to the last irreversible threshold of extremity.

So we will start closing this point with an accusation about a blind spot in the lines of questioning of contemporary thought, which is that it has somehow become fashionable to no longer consider existential variables with regard to subjectivity and the acute processes of becoming. Instead, on the one side, we have the terrible archetypal clichés of identitarianism, and on the other these mechanical "thinkers" who debate all such phenomena (black boxes, phantomologies) in a kind of ideal vacuum where there is no performative figure who will have to stake their lives on the wager. This is a terrible failure and cowardice in our chronicle of ideas—because we should not want to steal all the ingenuity and radical possibility of the thousand plateaus while skipping over the excruciating cost that rests beneath its table of contents; all the blood on the floor and the long nights of self-carving in order to be able to utter that earlier version of the term Black Box (which is the word "abyss"). All those texts about the violence, suffering, and ecstatic agony of becoming. One cannot skip steps; one cannot cheat the tightrope. One has no right to those terminologies unless doing the damned work and striking at the walls of being like a brutal ironsmith. To talk about the outside, one must first become the outsider; to dare answer riddles one must first risk being devoured by the Sphinx. Contemporary theorists often enjoy talking about phenomena and future and even the mind in a kind of mesmerizingly harmless bubble of forms, like some free-floating game without players. No, we must ask the untimely question, the same way that another interrogated us after the event of the death of God when probing: What must we murderers do to become worthy of the deed? Not to ask simply what is going to happen in the remote or near horizon and concoct trendy analytic jargons, but to ask the bare-bones question of what exactly is being demanded of us; what offerings enable one to live up to the futural occasion, and what in me might have to die here? This is the premise of monstrosity again: to ask the debt or the blood-price; what awful or awesome payment must we make in order to become something that can face the uneven?

But let us end very quickly on an affirmative proposition linked to this: If this becoming monster of the future is our imminent profile, then what kind of aberration are we dealing with, since every monster holds its own special power and influence? So does Lem write the following at the outset of his Phantomology chapter: "We shall ask, Is it possible to create an artificial reality that is very similar to the actual one yet that cannot be distinguished from it in any way? The first topic focuses on the creation of worlds, the second on the creation of illusions. But we are talking about perfect illusions."[77] Thus we are coming full circle to the question of the Pretender.

This sets us up to forge an elaborate proposal: for years many have been captivated by the concept of Hyperstition: i.e., the practice of converting fantastical ideas or suggestions into self-fulfilling prophecies in reality. But let us play around with the prospect of how one might execute a Reverse-Hyperstition: namely, could we imagine a shadow-figure of some kind whose touch would steal supposed realities back into the realms of the fictive and the illusory? A figure whose presence can disappear solid, authentic worlds into the mirage or hallucination? What if this is our ultimate challenge: to learn how to turn so-called realities unreal? And so we double back and bind together the three concepts of the pythonic, the enigmatic, and the monstrous: What if the shape-shifter just mentioned does this as a kind of vengeance on behalf of all those contrary selves, forfeited tasks, and overlooked conceivable worlds that hang in some invisible exile of time? Is this yet another subtext of Night?

Epilogue: The Last King

Many know the story of The Last King, though somehow each tells it differently and in their own diverging way. A shadow-motif or undercurrent, something that haunts the cellar corners of world thought every now and again. Still, two details remain consistent in the recurring imagination of this figure across millennia: night and desert (or rather, that he rules the night-desert).

Time. Some claim that he descends from an ancient race and is possessed of accursed immortality, thus tying the desert to a philosophy of punishment and of the undead, though within that same narrative branch are disagreements as to whether his torment arose from being a great traitor or an innocent. Others claim that he arrives from the future as a retroactive reckoning, or even from an inconceivable hypothetical temporality that never materialized, thus tying the desert to a philosophy of vindictive potentiality. And still others spread rumors that he persists mournfully through fractional arrangements of milliseconds in which he is constantly made to die (with every supposed blinking of his eyes).

Affect. Some say he is tortured internally and leads a destiny of inexorable suffering, while others depict him as a sadistic phantom who delights in the agony of nomads and desperate souls. Some attribute the sound of nocturnal winds to him, others the alignment of the night stars, and still others the shifting of the sands in the dark into ominous coiling shapes.

Language. Some say his eternality binds him to a code of silence, while others say that he talks to himself nonstop in delirious run-on sentences, and still others believe that he speaks in the lost letters of the first alphabet (stolen phonetics of the origin). Still another minority claims that his only recourse to language altogether is the writing of death-sentences on small scraps of paper that then seal events into disastrous finality.

Appearance. Some say he resembles a wraith equipped with sharpened implements, while others focus on the details of his kingly accessories—robe, scepter, diadem, ring—while still others concentrate their imagination on his wistful movements (hovering, slouching) or on particular physiological features, organs, or deformities (hollowed eye sockets, elongated fingernails, fanged teeth, disheveled hair, disproportionate height or bone structure). Still, some alternative schools note that his body coats itself in the symbols of every overthrown dynasty in history, thus tying the night-desert to the long line of failed utopias behind and ahead of our mortal experiment.

Sighting 1: Babylon, 539 BC. For certain, there are many examples of The Last King across various regions of storytelling, philosophy, myth, and aesthetics. The Babylonian lord Nabonidus essentially forfeited his empire to the Persians by default, allowing his inexperienced son to manage the capital while he obsessively roamed the desert building temples to the moon god Sin. His fanaticism led him away from the center and into the scorched-earth periphery to honor a lunar-mirage metaphysics. Study the equation: Night, Desert, Last King. Thus the sequence sets itself in motion, and the first civilizations fall.

Sighting 2: Palestine, 1994. Thousands of years later in a trampled land not far from Babylon, the poet Mahmoud Darwish will declare that, "I am one of the kings of the end," thereby resurrecting the dream of the Last King in a time of war, disappearance, and the lost cause. He refers to himself as a tragi-multiplied version of the Edenic Adam, this one being of two broken gardens "who lost paradise twice" and now requests only to "expel me slowly, kill me slowly."[78] Catastrophically, the night-desert is also long-known for granting such wishes.

Sighting 3: Paris, 1892. An eccentric French writer named Joséphin Péladan forms an aristocratic secret society and mystical order—*The Salon de la Rose + Croix*—devoted to explorations of esoteric-occult representation in art. He appoints himself a high priest and mage and goes by the magisterial title of *Sâr* which he claims was handed down to his family (his own father a scholar of prognostications) by a Babylonian emperor, spending the next decade initiating Symbolist painters in an untimely style whose content often gravitates toward damned or murdered mythic figures (i.e., resurrections of forgotten sovereigns).

Sighting 4: Austria, 1902. Hidden away in another obscure recess of artistic curiosity, in the dim-lit studio of a modest illustrator of grim fantastical scenes, we stare upon the drawing of Alfred Kubin's *The Last King*. His black-and-white protagonist is shown seated on an oversized, rounded throne whose arms engulf from both sides; he wears a delicate lace costume of exaggerated sleeves and collars, and slippers with tipped points. His frame is eerily slender (almost skeletal) and his visage angular in the shape of extraterrestrial beings; he is inconceivably pale, and stares downward into nothing with large glazed eyelids. His crown is a simple minimalist halo of metallic spikes, and he is swarmed beneath his feet by crowds of heavy-robed subjects burning incense and looking away (anywhere but toward the face of their king). For it is the look of the ultimate deserter they avoid: the one who, while still presumably here, has already long since gone from this world.

Sightings 5, 6, 7: Mexico, 1952, 1955; United Kingdom, 1974. In rarer instances, the story revolves around the image of the Last Queen, who often combines majesty and disfigurement like the Gorgon royalty Medusa. Indeed, her snake-filled hair was also a token of the night-desert's at once short-lived wrath and ominous longevity. For the Last Queen is appalling; she is the appalling itself, with wisdom enough to know that we are caught in an unwise existence. So it is that three extraordinary outcast women of the Surrealist circle—Remedios Varo, Leonora Carrington, and Ithell Colquhoun—would find themselves drawn to the feminine manifestations of this conceptual character. While some ethereal visual allusions of the Last Queen can be spotted in Varo's renderings of *The Hermit, Star Huntress, Insomniac II, Night Spirit, Red Weaver,* and *Dragonfly Woman* (all solitary, irreproducible astral personifications), we find others spread throughout Carrington's *The Magical World of the Mayans* (referencing an extinct civilization) alongside her *And Then We Saw the Daughter of the Minotaur!* (referencing an extinct fabled species), only then to encounter Colquhoun's *Princess of the Echoing Hills* (with its imperial subject fading into a whirlpool of color and abstraction). Nevertheless, a little-known fact to bind these three artistic forerunners is that they all found themselves designers of unique Tarot Decks. These artifacts are the exemplars of a disturbing genius: one can search for such mesmerizing fortune-telling items, each playing card drawing thematically from the sinister potentialities of the ancient Egyptian night-desert. Thus it is Colquhoun who writes of the Empress card:

> Like the Woman of the Apocalypse, the Empress wears a crown of 12 stars in the form of hexagrams to show that she has dominion over the laws of the macrocosm...The gates on her headdress are 7, corresponding to the 7 houses of her celestial mansion = 7 planets. The Serpent symbol occurs in each doorway...for the Serpents guard the gates.[79]

Apparently, these iterations of The Last Queen are also intimately linked to the architectonic principles of the underworld and to the formulae of future becomings.

Sightings 8, 9: Iran/New York City, 2010-2015. Our last two examples of these curtain-call despots are by two Iranian women artists in exile—Shiva Ahmadi and Shirin Neshat—who lived through the macabre political theater of an anti-monarchical revolution. They are therefore witnesses of a certain kind to the anti-climactic sagas of an actual last king, both its poisonous reign and poisoned aftermath. Hence, whereas the former depicts faceless sultans atop golden thrones covered in blood, their own flesh and torsos bathed in red streaking wounds, the latter's exhibition titled *The Book of Kings: Villains Series* assembles a file of shirtless men of differing ages with sprawling battle scenes from epic Persian literature (hunting, archery, martial swordplay) tattooed across their chests. Both are powerful commentaries on the drained evocative energy of these emblems in an age of disenchantment but also of the violence-patterned universe that always lurked beneath the towers, castles, and court ceremonies. Millennial disgrace.

Unfortunately, this is where the story of The Last King/Queen becomes complicated by a juncture of three forking paths: For what is the lesson derived from this apparition of the nocturnal and the wasteland? Faction 1: Regimania (love of the king). Faction 2: Regiphobia (fear of the king). Faction 3: Regicide (killing of the king). The first camp clings to these parables as evidence of an allegorical return: namely, that the concluding regent in fact constitutes the last chance of the world itself and the prospect of reversal from an epoch of despair, havoc, and technological malice. The temporality of these Last King/Queen followers is therefore one of the eleventh hour (urgent search for the exception); their movements are infused by avant-gardism (militant resurgence); their identity-structures are characterized by that of the descendant (legacy, gift); their methods are archetypal and ritualistic; their atmospheric states are those of ecstasy, awe, hallowing, and lamentation.

The second school of thought, however, revolves around a more diabolical reading of The Last King/Queen as end-times force: namely, they are overridden by fearful suspicion and see nothing in this figure's countenance save the unstoppable designation of the collapse. Not a trace of heroic or merciful nobility, but rather only a quick-blade instrument of fatalistic eventuality; this other is therefore the practitioner, executioner, and enforcer of negative will in its most perilous sense; it administrates the logistics of devastation's last laugh. Doomsday consciousness: This is when future becomes pure night, pure desert, against all odds and efforts, for The Last King/Queen graces the halls only when struggle quits reality itself and submits hope to the hangman. The temporality of these Last King/Queen whisperers is therefore one of lateness (irreversibility, massacre); their movements have a tinge of apocalyptic decadence (futility); their identity-structures are characterized by that of the elegist and the reciter; their methods are those of useless warning, horror tale, mockery, sneering, or the fool's farewell toast; their atmospheric states are those of exhaustion, trembling, spite, and absurd resignation.

But then there is the third faction, perhaps the strangest and most impressive of all interpretive chambers: for here there are also lingering tidings of possibility, but consummated only through the elevation of a single imperative above all others—Regicide. More precisely, these are a warlike cadre who perceive their lone escape-route in the murdered heart of The Last King/Queen. The colossus must be undone or burnt, for this alone restores tranquility or even futurity to the night-desert. Consequently, this circle's temporality is one of criminal interruption and radical betrayal; their movements are showered in disciplined spells of subversion and plots of conspiratorial puncture; their identity-structures are conceived around hoods of the enemy and the assassin; their methods are those of effigy, vandalism, sabotage, stealth, and guillotine; their atmospheric states are those of neutrality, coldness, necessity, and cosmic vengeance.

All of these are blood-debts, to be sure. For the desert always asks for more than it gives; the night always demands more than it offers; the future always promises more than it delivers. This is the preordinate rule of a bad game (illusory excess)—one that children, animals, and ghosts detect all too well but which for all others the precipice of a barren world remains hidden behind a delusional impulse to rule for all time. The absolute absolves nothing. This is why the temptation to last forever must be overturned by the last king or queen, whether through their blood-seeking or blood-letting, their cruelty or their sacrifice, as if writing the manual for a future desert with their own dried veins. And all this in order to fulfill the badland's prophecy once and for all (whether that of the sandstorm, the oasis, or the night sky).

Endnotes

Chapter 1 originally published as "Into Night (Five Rooms at the End of the World" in *Interior Realms* eds. Andrea Cetrulo and Marta Michalowska (London: Theatrum Mundi, 2021).

Chapter 2 originally published as "Night and Silence (Five Breaths at the End of the World)" in *Silence and Silencing in History, Language, and Culture* eds. Mahshid Mayar and Marion Schulte (New York: Palgrave Macmillan, 2021).

Chapter 3 originally published as "Night and Violence (Five Raids at the End of the World)" in *A Glossary for the XXI Century* eds. Michael Marder and Giovanni Tusa (London: Bloomsbury, 2021).

Chapter 4 originally published as "Night and Secrecy (Five Sects at the End of the World)" in *Acéphale and Autobiographical Philosophy in the 21st Century* eds. Edia Connole and Gary J. Shipley (Schism Press, 2021).

Interlude 1 originally composed as two essays for the False Mirror (Sacred Hill) virtual reality project and the Nerd_Funk art installation project with artists Ali Eslami, Klasien van de Zandschulp, and Mamali Shafahi (Amsterdam, 2021).

Interlude 2 originally published as an interview with Dana Dawud titled "Restraint: Between Fire and the Labyrinth" in *The Derivative: Issue 12/01/2020*.

Interlude 3 originally published as "Philosophy of the Fallen: On Kafka's Savage" in Hyperion: On the Future of Aesthetics Journal (Volume XIII, Issue No. 1), 2020.

Interlude 4 originally presented at the *Summa Technolologiae Seminars* (e-flux and the Adam Mickiewicz Institute, 2020).

Epilogue originally published as "The Last King" for *Manual for a Future Desert* eds. Bassam El Baroni, Abinadi Meza, and Ida Soulard (Milan: Mousse Publishing, 2021).

1. Haruki Murakami, *After Dark* (New York: Vintage, 2008), 186.
2. Jorge Luis Borges, "A History of the Night" in *Poems of the Night* (New York: Penguin, 2010).
3. Griselda Gambaro, "Scene 12" in *Information for Foreigners: Three Plays* (Evanston: Northwestern University Press, 1992).
4. Unica Zurn, *The Man of Jasmine & Other Texts* (London: Atlas Press, 1994), 25.
5. Mahmoud al-Buraikan, "Tale of the Assyrian Statue" in *Modern Arabic Poetry: An Anthology* ed. Salma Khadra Jayussi (New York: Columbia University Press, 1987), 188.
6. Gaston Bachelard, *The Poetics of Reverie* (Boston: Beacon Press, 1971), 147.
7. Maurice Blanchot, *The Space of Literature* (Lincoln: University of Nebraska Press, 1989), 116.
8. Margaret Atwood, *Selected Poems II: Poems Selected & New 1976-1986* (Boston: Houghton Mifflin, 1987): 52.
9. Roger Gilbert-Lecomte, "Into the Eyes of Night" in *Black Mirror* (Barrytown: Station Hill Press, 2010), 89.
10. Ahmed Bouanani, *The Hospital* trans. L. Vergnaud (New York: New Directions, 2018), 37.
11. Bouanani, 39.
12. Bouanani, 39.
13. Bouanani, 42.
14. Vi Khi Nao. "The Boy and The Mountain" in *A Brief Alphabet of Torture* (Tuscaloosa: The University of Alabama Press, 2017), 113.
15. Vi Khi Nao, 114.
16. Vi Khi Nao, 106.
17. The forerunners in cognitive studies on schizophrenia's pertinence to temporal discrepancy, which include measuring critical fusion frequencies of individual memory, reaction time, and retroactive perception while in states of

terror-spiking (e.g. roller-coaster rides), can be found at the following: Stetson, C., Fiesta, M.P., & Eagleman, D.M. Does time really slow down during a frightening event? *PLoS One* 2, e1295 (2007); Parsons, B.D., *et al.* Lengthened temporal integration in schizophrenia. *Neuropsychologia* 51, 372–376 (2013).

18. Vi Khi Nao, 115.
19. Vi Khi Nao, 137.
20. Alejandra Pizarnik, *Extraction of the Madness Stone* (1968) trans. E. Ruiz (Duquesne University): (https://www.academia.edu/26544858/Extracci%C3%B3n_de_la_piedra_de_la_locura_Extraction_of_the_Madness_Stone_by_Alejandra_Pizarnik), 18.
21. Ibid., 12.
22. Ibid., 18.
23. Alejandra Pizarnik, "Cornerstone" in *Extracting the Stones of Madness* trans. Y. Siegert (New York: New Directions, 2016).
24. Pizarnik (1968), 12.
25. Pizarnik (1968), 14.
26. Pizarnik (1968), 4.
27. Pizarnik (1968), 5.
28. Pizarnik (1968), 5.
29. Pizarnik (1968), 5, 6.
30. Pizarnik (1968), 5.
31. Pizarnik (1968), 5.
32. Hélène Cixous, *Three Steps on the Ladder of Writing* trans. S. Sellers (New York: Columbia University Press, 1994), 122.
33. Cixous, 120.
34. Cixous, 65.
35. Clarice Lispector in Cixous, 104.
36. Cixous, 65.
37. Cixous, 105.
38. Cixous, 105.

39. Kobo Abe, *The Box Man* trans. E.D. Saunders (New York: Vintage, 2001), 14 [e-book version].
40. See Morgan L. Kaplan, "Death Dust: The Little-Known Story of US and Soviet Pursuit of Radiological Weapons" (The MIT Press Reader, 2020).
41. Abe, 47.
42. Kobo Abe, *The Face of Another* trans. E.D. Saunders (New York: Vintage, 2003).
43. Giorgio Manganelli, *To Those Gods Beyond* trans. M. McLaughlin (London: Atlas Press, 2019), 104-106.
44. Manganelli, 19.
45. Ibid., 45.
46. Ibid., 96.
47. Ibid., 96.
48. Ibid., 174.
49. Estamira Gomes de Souza in *Estamira* (film), Director: Marcos Prado (2004).
50. Gaston Bachelard, *Air and Dreams: An Essay on the Imagination of Movement* (Dallas: The Dallas Institute Publications, 1970), 157, 160.
51. Al-Khadra Mint Mabrook, "Al-Khadra: Poet of the Desert" in *Poets of Protest Series* (Artscape: Al-Jazeera, 2012).
52. Vladimir Bartol, *Alamut* trans. M. Biggins (Berkeley: North Atlantic Books, 2007), 51.
53. Georges Bataille, "On an area of marshy ground . . . ," in Georges Bataille, et alia, *The Sacred Conspiracy: The Internal Papers of the Secret Society of Acéphale and Lectures to the College of Sociology*, ed. Marina Galletti and Alastair Brotchie, trans. Natasha Lehrer, John Harman, and Meyer Barash (London: Atlas Press, 2017), 179.
54. Bataille, "The Practice of Joy in the Face of Death" in *The Sacred Conspiracy*, 434-435.
55. Bataille, 454.
56. Henri Dussat, "Meditation before the Cross" in *The Sacred*

Conspiracy, 240.

57. Dussat, 240-241.

58. Dussat, "Meditation in the Forest" in *The Sacred Conspiracy*, 266.

59. The spiritual and paranormal uses of Aconitum ferox (also known as Bish, monkshood, wolf's bane, leopard's bane, women's bane, the Devil's Helmet, and Queen of All Poisons) were originally pointed out to me in a private conversation with Reza Negarestani. [03-18-2021]

60. Michel Leiris, "The Sacred in Everyday Life" in *The Sacred Conspiracy*, 281.

61. Leiris, 279.

62. Leiris, 282.

63. Leiris, 282.

64. Leiris, 281.

65. Roger Caillois, "Theory of the Festival" in *The Sacred Conspiracy*, 390.

66. Caillois, 384.

67. Caillois, 383.

68. Caillois, 394.

69. Caillois, 395.

70. See Maurice Blanchot, *The Space of Literature* (University of Nebraska Press, 1989).

71. Friedrich Nietzsche, *The Portable Nietzsche* trans. W. Kaufmann, "On the Vision and the Riddle" in *Thus Spoke Zarathustra* (New York: Penguin, 1977), 158.

72. Pierre Klossowski, "The Monster" in *The Sacred Conspiracy*, 129.

73. This "philosophy of the fallen" is also predicated on tracing the connection between Night and the concept of the Abyss in lesser-known domains of thought.

74. The chosen term here is misleading in that it is typically "the barbarian" (not "the savage") who by definition constitutes the enemy of civilization. The savage generally exists

in non-relation to the rising cities, of which they remain unaware, whereas the barbarian harbors a clear vendetta: the latter looks to storm the high gates and burn all palaces as some terrorizing negation of the emergent epoch. To this end, Kafka does extend an accursed quality to his legion—later in the same piece he writes that they are "dreaded as though they were the Devil"—yet this is simply an inadvertent mood that emanates from their self-enveloped practice. They do not actually ride against the walls of the real but rather evacuate their own survival-instinct (a first primal criterion), offering no resistance to lethal capture by the undertow. They fight nothing, not even the nothing itself, and still somehow embody an awful severity. Does this speak to another ancestral destiny, then, based neither in the savage's oblivion nor the barbarian's hatred? What should we call this will to slowest immersion—itself an amalgam of extreme fatalism, endurance, and vulnerability? Have they studied the logic of the whirlpool itself, manifest in this exceptional vigilance, this long-gone subject that conveys itself to the drift if only to threaten the collapse of worlds?

75. Stanislaw Lem, *Summa Technologiae* trans. Joanna Zylinska (Minneapolis, University of Minnesota Press: 2013), 3.

76. Ibid., 90.

77. Ibid., 191.

78. Mahmoud Darwish, "Eleven Planets at the End of the Andalusian Scene" in *If I Were Another* trans. F. Joudah (New York: Farrar, Strauss, and Giroux, 2009), 59-60.

79. Ithell Colquhoun, *The Magical Writings of Ithell Colquhoun* ed. Steve Nichols (2020).

CULTURE, SOCIETY & POLITICS

The modern world is at an impasse. Disasters scroll across our smartphone screens and we're invited to like, follow or upvote, but critical thinking is harder and harder to find. Rather than connecting us in common struggle and debate, the internet has sped up and deepened a long-standing process of alienation and atomization. Zer0 Books wants to work against this trend. With critical theory as our jumping off point, we aim to publish books that make our readers uncomfortable. We want to move beyond received opinions.

Zer0 Books is on the left and wants to reinvent the left. We are sick of the injustice, the suffering and the stupidity that defines both our political and cultural world, and we aim to find a new foundation for a new struggle.

If this book has helped you to clarify an idea, solve a problem or extend your knowledge, you may want to check out our online content as well. Look for Zer0 Books: Advancing Conversations in the iTunes directory and for our Zer0 Books YouTube channel.

Popular videos include:

Žižek and the Double Blackmain

The Intellectual Dark Web is a Bad Sign

Can there be an Anti-SJW Left?

Answering Jordan Peterson on Marxism

Follow us on Facebook
at https://www.facebook.com/ZeroBooks and Twitter at https://
twitter.com/Zer0Books

Bestsellers from Zer0 Books include:

Give Them An Argument
Logic for the Left
Ben Burgis
Many serious leftists have learned to distrust talk of logic. This is
a serious mistake.
Paperback: 978-1-78904-210-8 ebook: 978-1-78904-211-5

Poor but Sexy
Culture Clashes in Europe East and West
Agata Pyzik
How the East stayed East and the West stayed West.
Paperback: 978-1-78099-394-2 ebook: 978-1-78099-395-9

An Anthropology of Nothing in Particular
Martin Demant Frederiksen
A journey into the social lives of meaninglessness.
Paperback: 978-1-78535-699-5 ebook: 978-1-78535-700-8

In the Dust of This Planet
Horror of Philosophy vol. 1
Eugene Thacker
In the first of a series of three books on the Horror of Philosophy,
In the Dust of This Planet offers the genre of horror as a way of
thinking about the unthinkable.
Paperback: 978-1-84694-676-9 ebook: 978-1-78099-010-1

The End of Oulipo?
An Attempt to Exhaust a Movement
Lauren Elkin, Veronica Esposito
Paperback: 978-1-78099-655-4 ebook: 978-1-78099-656-1

Capitalist Realism
Is There No Alternative?
Mark Fisher
An analysis of the ways in which capitalism has presented itself
as the only realistic political-economic system.
Paperback: 978-1-84694-317-1 ebook: 978-1-78099-734-6

Rebel Rebel
Chris O'Leary
David Bowie: every single song. Everything you want to know,
everything you didn't know.
Paperback: 978-1-78099-244-0 ebook: 978-1-78099-713-1

Kill All Normies
Angela Nagle
Online culture wars from 4chan and Tumblr to Trump.
Paperback: 978-1-78535-543-1 ebook: 978-1-78535-544-8

Cartographies of the Absolute
Alberto Toscano, Jeff Kinkle
An aesthetics of the economy for the twenty-first century.
Paperback: 978-1-78099-275-4 ebook: 978-1-78279-973-3

Malign Velocities
Accelerationism and Capitalism
Benjamin Noys
Long listed for the Bread and Roses Prize 2015, *Malign Velocities*
argues against the need for speed, tracking acceleration
as the symptom of the ongoing crises of capitalism.
Paperback: 978-1-78279-300-7 ebook: 978-1-78279-299-4

Meat Market
Female Flesh under Capitalism
Laurie Penny
A feminist dissection of women's bodies as the fleshy fulcrum of
capitalist cannibalism, whereby women are both consumers and
consumed.
Paperback: 978-1-84694-521-2 ebook: 978-1-84694-782-7

Babbling Corpse
Vaporwave and the Commodification of Ghosts
Grafton Tanner
Paperback: 978-1-78279-759-3 ebook: 978-1-78279-760-9

New Work New Culture
Work we want and a culture that strengthens us
Frithjof Bergmann
A serious alternative for mankind and the planet.
Paperback: 978-1-78904-064-7 ebook: 978-1-78904-065-4

Romeo and Juliet in Palestine
Teaching Under Occupation
Tom Sperlinger
Life in the West Bank, the nature of pedagogy and the role of a
university under occupation.
Paperback: 978-1-78279-637-4 ebook: 978-1-78279-636-7

Ghosts of My Life
Writings on Depression, Hauntology and Lost Futures
Mark Fisher
Paperback: 978-1-78099-226-6 ebook: 978-1-78279-624-4

Sweetening the Pill
or How We Got Hooked on Hormonal Birth Control
Holly Grigg-Spall
Has contraception liberated or oppressed women?
Sweetening the Pill breaks the silence on the dark side of hormonal
contraception.
Paperback: 978-1-78099-607-3 ebook: 978-1-78099-608-0

Why Are We The Good Guys?
Reclaiming Your Mind from the Delusions of Propaganda
David Cromwell
A provocative challenge to the standard ideology that Western
power is a benevolent force in the world.
Paperback: 978-1-78099-365-2 ebook: 978-1-78099-366-9

The Writing on the Wall
On the Decomposition of Capitalism and its Critics
Anselm Jappe, Alastair Hemmens
A new approach to the meaning of social emancipation.
Paperback: 978-1-78535-581-3 ebook: 978-1-78535-582-0

Enjoying It
Candy Crush and Capitalism
Alfie Bown
A study of enjoyment and of the enjoyment of studying. Bown
asks what enjoyment says about us and what we say about
enjoyment, and why.
Paperback: 978-1-78535-155-6 ebook: 978-1-78535-156-3

Color, Facture, Art and Design
Iona Singh
This materialist definition of fine-art develops guidelines for
architecture, design, cultural-studies and ultimately social
change.
Paperback: 978-1-78099-629-5 ebook: 978-1-78099-630-1

Neglected or Misunderstood
The Radical Feminism of Shulamith Firestone
Victoria Margree
An interrogation of issues surrounding gender, biology,
sexuality, work and technology, and the ways in which our
imaginations continue to be in thrall to ideologies of maternity
and the nuclear family.
Paperback: 978-1-78535-539-4 ebook: 978-1-78535-540-0

How to Dismantle the NHS in 10 Easy Steps (Second Edition)
Youssef El-Gingihy
The story of how your NHS was sold off and why you will have
to buy private health insurance soon. A new expanded second
edition with chapters on junior doctors' strikes and government
blueprints for US-style healthcare.
Paperback: 978-1-78904-178-1 ebook: 978-1-78904-179-8

Digesting Recipes
The Art of Culinary Notation
Susannah Worth
A recipe is an instruction, the imperative tone of the expert, but
this constraint can offer its own kind of potential. A recipe need
not be a domestic trap but might instead offer escape – something
to fantasise about or aspire to.
Paperback: 978-1-78279-860-6 ebook: 978-1-78279-859-0

Most titles are published in paperback and as an ebook.
Paperbacks are available in traditional bookshops. Both print and
ebook formats are available online.
Follow us on Facebook
at https://www.facebook.com/ZeroBooks
and Twitter at https://twitter.com/Zer0Books